From Fear to Faith

A Family's Journey with Addiction, Recovery, and Grace

Lisa and Hans Scheller

Joshua Tree Publishing

• Chicago •

From Fear to Faith

A Family's Journey with Addiction, Recovery, and Grace

Lisa and Hans Scheller

Joshua Tree
Publishing

Published by
Joshua Tree Publishing
• Chicago •
JoshuaTreePublishing.com

13-Digit ISBN: 978-1-956823-16-5

Front Cover Credit: Luke Powell. Indiana Dunes National Park
Back Cover Photo: Estero Beach, Florida

Disclaimer:
This book is designed to provide information about the subject matter covered. The opinions and information expressed in this book are those of the author, not the publisher. Every effort has been made to make this book as complete and as accurate as possible. However, there may be mistakes both typographical and in content. Therefore, this text should be used only as a general guide and not as the ultimate source of information. The author and publisher of this book shall have neither liability nor responsibility to any person or entity with respect to any loss or damage caused or alleged to be caused directly or indirectly by the information contained in this book.

Printed in the United States of America

Dedication

To all those that are struggling or have struggled through alcoholism and addiction. We were you, and we know God has you covered with his own plan. Our family is *so* thankful and has so much gratitude to our community of family and friends who have walked our journey with us. Those who were there without judgment or expectations and who loved us unconditionally.

To our amazing girls, Hannah and Delaney, for being adaptable to our family's ever-changing journey. For being the beautiful, talented, loving, compassionate, and caring ladies you are. We are very proud of both of you for keeping your head up; for being positive when it would have been easier to keep it down; and for doing your part by studying hard, making good friends, and being Christ-like and always caring young ladies. Thank you for sharing your journey and for being a friend to those in need. Love you both all around the world millions and millions and millions!

Table of Contents

About Lisa and Hans

L isa grew up in St. Cloud, Minnesota. She attended Minnesota State University in Mankato, Minnesota, where she earned a bachelor of science degree in social work. Lisa has worked in the nonprofit world for over thirty years—dedicating herself to the mission of several amazing organizations. Lisa is an entrepreneur by nature, owning several of her own businesses. Lisa also is a certified health coach through the Institute for Integrative Nutrition as well as a certified professional family recovery coach, certified professional nutritional recovery coach, and relapse prevention coach through the Addictions Academy.

Living a life dealing with alcohol addiction of a loved one was the furthest thing from Lisa's mind when she moved to Valparaiso, Indiana, twenty-three years ago to start her new life and a future family. Lisa wants the readers to know that her family is your neighbor next door. While everything may look wonderful on the outside—a beautiful big house, a successful small business, two amazing daughters, an awesome community of friends, a wonderful church family, and a dedicated husband—you can be blindsided and your life turned upside down when stress and life events take over your marriage.

* * *

Hans was born in West Germany and moved to the United States when he was three years old. His formative years were relatively typical while living with his family—sports, college, and jobs. His alcoholism did not manifest itself until his late thirties, when a series of detrimental life events occurred. He has overcome alcoholism, three suicide attempts, three inpatient periods in rehab, his sister's death from a drug overdose, and a lengthy stay at a halfway house along with numerous other obstacles culminating in a fulfilling life. He is a certified peer recovery coach, personnel manager at an injection molding company, as well as a dedicated, loving father and husband. This collaboration with his wife, Lisa, stems from the strong desire to help others who find themselves in a similar situation by providing clarity, support, direction, and most importantly, *hope.*

* * *

Lisa and Hans believe their family's addiction journey and story is a gift given to them from God to share with others in which they can provide support, encouragement, and a listening ear to those who are walking the same dark journey their family has walked. As a very close friend, Gary, once told Lisa along the journey, "This is the valley of darkness. These are the details of life. You will come through on the other side. God already knows your story, and he loves you."

Lisa and Hans have their own coaching business, Heart and Health, offering their services to those who want to get back on track. They help those who need someone who can understand them and their family's situation without judgment and meet them where they are in their own lives.

Lisa and Hans reside in Chesterton, Indiana, with their two daughters, Hannah and Delaney, who both attend Valparaiso University. They also live with their three dogs: Polly, Penelope, and Posie. Their family loves spending time together camping, going to church, traveling, enjoying the outdoors, serving others, and just being together.

Hans, Polly, Delaney, Posie, Hannah, Penelope Lisa

Acknowledgments

Writing this book about our family journey has been a surreal experience. We are forever indebted to the following family and friends who walked with us providing encouragement and support in which we are able to leave a legacy to pass on to our family and community.

Lisa's sister Sheila, who always answered the phone call and was there to remind Lisa to keep moving forward even when it seemed easier to give up. Sheila reminded Lisa often that though this was a road untraveled, they were going to be okay. Thank you, Sheila, for always sticking by us. Love you more than you will ever know!

Lisa's dad—Hannah and Delaney's Papa—Duane Olson, for having been only a phone call away and having the door always open. We miss you! (Lisa's dad passed away on February 17, 2020.)

Lisa's mom—Hannah and Delaney's Granny—Shirley Olson, who is an angel in heaven watching over us and guiding us every step of the way. Thank you for always reminding us of your presence. Love you!

Brian and Marlo Harding, we are truly blessed beyond words that God placed you all in our family in our darkest days. There are no words for the gratitude we feel for all that you both did for us as well as your extended family. No judgment, just *love*! Love you both!

Lisa's village mommas and besties—Michele Gustin, Colleen Dumelle, Lisa Joesten, Kim Maggio, Sandy Young, and all the other mommas who stepped in to care for Hannah and Delaney or were just a phone call away. I am truly blessed with your forever friendship, encouragement, support, and love. I am so thankful God placed each one of you in my life and our family's life. I don't know how I could ever repay you for being there for us unconditionally and for standing in the gap when we needed you the most. Love you all *so* much!

Carolyn Hughes, for being the friend who was there for Hannah at Camp Lawrence and making sure a gentle message was given to her about her dad. Thank you for always being there for both Hannah and Delaney. Love you!

Eric and Kristen Mathisen, for opening their home to Hans when he returned from Southern Indiana, with no questions or judgment, only love and acceptance! Thank you for your friendship, your prayers, and your faith in our family.

Indiana Dunes Great Banquet Community, for their prayers and agape love. It's because of our sisters and brothers in Christ that we could get through each day one at a time. Thank you for wrapping our family in love and for just being there. We love you all!

Chris and Monica Hoham, plus their extended family, for opening their home to us not once but twice for as long as we needed a roof over our heads. For sharing your holidays with us and for just being the unselfish friends that you are. We cannot thank you all enough for walking our journey with us and reminding us that we were always where we were supposed to be along the way.

Gary and Beth Germann, for showing our family what it truly meant to be the hands and feet for others. For being there when we were in our darkest days and giving us hope to keep walking through it because we were going to come out on the other side stronger. Thank you, Gary, for always being a phone call away. Thank you to Beth for sitting with Lisa at church when she needed a friend the most. Mostly, thank you for your *love* and friendship.

Molly Sabourin, for her beautiful friendship, her positive encouragement to keep moving forward, her generous love for our family, and her inspiration to keep the book going when Lisa had her doubts. Molly would say, "Someone out there needs to hear your story, and it is God's will for you to share it. You are going to make a difference in someone's life and family." Love you, Molly!

Wayne Rhodes, for the constant encouragement and friendship you have so graciously given to Hans over the years. Thank you for your continued prayers and unselfish love but mostly for believing in Hans.

Thorgren Family—for being a huge *blessing* to our family. There are no words that can express our deepest gratitude to you all. You have changed our family's lives for the better, and for this, we are *so thankful*! Love you all!

Bob Jennings, for being a friend, adviser, and spiritual guide at all times!

Jon and Amber Hicks, for constant support and enthusiasm. Jon provided constructive feedback about the book as well as decades of friendship, and Amber provided Hans with his first *Life Recovery Bible*, which is now blessedly dog-eared and treasured.

Kevin and Tami Maxey, thank you both for being the light in our darkness. Thank you for praying for us, standing in the gap, and wrapping your arms around us with only love and acceptance. We love you both!

Ken and Heather Crews, for always being there for our family no matter what. For always being positive and encouraging as well as setting examples for both Hannah and Delaney. Love you both!

Gretchen Gibbs, thank you for always being a phone call away and making time for Lisa, for giving sound advice, and for your continued prayers for our family. You were exactly where you were supposed to be in the midst of our family's darkness, and for this we are forever grateful to you!

Jeanne Ann Cannon, thank you for not only being a fabulous boss but more an amazing friend and mentor to Lisa. The last two years of your friendship has brought me SO much joy and laughter. Thank you for believing in me and for always being only a phone call away anytime. I am forever blessed God put you in my life. Love you!

Testimonials

What an honor to be able to encourage you to read, to listen, and to learn about the story of two dear friends of mine, Lisa and Hans. In retrospect, it was amazing to me to have been friends with Hans and Lisa and never really see the life's struggles with which they were dealing on an everyday basis. While the story is still being written, I cannot imagine what their story would look like today without the healing power of the Lord Jesus Christ, their faith in Him, and their faith and devotion in His love to each other. Hans and Lisa inspire me, and I hope you too will be inspired by their story of faith, restoration, and redemption. It really is an honor.

Love,
Gary

Dear Lisa and Hans, you both are the answer to our prayers! You came along when we did not know where to turn and completely loved and encouraged us. May our Lord and Savior richly bless you for your kindness!

Love,
John and Tonya

Lisa, you are a true blessing. I am not sure where I would be if it wasn't for you and your listening ear. Talking to you is a gift like no other . . . There is no judgment, you understand, and there is nothing I could say that would surprise you. Thank you for being a phone call away always.

Love,
Mary

When Hans and Lisa Met

Lisa

Meeting Hans

We don't meet people by accident; they are
meant to cross our paths.

W hile at the Boys & Girls Clubs of Central Minnesota, I attended several conferences that brought many club professionals together for youth development seminars, club supervision, management, and so on from different clubs in the Midwest. As with any professional conference, there was lots of networking. In October of 1996, I attended a conference in Milwaukee when some of us from St. Cloud met some of the staff from Valparaiso, Indiana. Hans was among this group. They were a fun group, and we would hang out in the evening after a full day of seminars. We all had a great time socializing, learning from each other, and making new friends. After another great conference, we went back to our clubs and implemented the wonderful things we'd learned.

A year later, October 1997, I attended a Boys & Girls Clubs conference in Indianapolis. There weren't plans for anyone to attend the conference from St. Cloud, but at the very last minute, one of my coworkers and I decided to go. As always, it was great to see so many friends we met over the years. I was excited to catch up with people I hadn't seen for a while. Once again, I saw Hans and his coworkers. We spent the days in seminars and the evenings socializing. At these conferences, there were many fun evening events to participate in. One was a visit to tour a local club. I happened to sit on the bus with Hans. We started talking about life in general. He shared with me that his wife did not want children and he was not happy in his relationship. He talked about a trip he was going to take with his wife and their best friends. The conversation ended when we got back to the hotel. Hans and I went our separate ways.

That evening there was an awards dinner for all the participants. I found myself sitting at a table next to Hans, who asked if I wanted a drink, and I said, "Sure." He was such a gentleman. I really didn't think much more about it. After dinner, a group of us went to a local bar, played darts and pool, laughed, and had a great time. The weekend came to an end, and we all said our goodbyes and went back home.

A couple of weeks later, out of the blue, I received a call from Hans.

I heard on the other end, "Hi, how are you?"

"Good," I said.

"Are you good, really?" Hans asked.

We talked for just a few minutes that night. Hans was in Valparaiso doing life, and he was not happy in his marriage. I was in Minnesota, married, and was not happy. Life was not going the way I had planned. My husband and I had good jobs and a new beautiful house to move in to, but things were just not right. I was in my mid-thirties, and I knew time was running out for me to have the natural family I'd always dreamed of.

I constantly questioned, "Why was God letting me down? Why are we not being blessed with a family?"

During this time, I believed God would take care of me. I am a planner. My job has always been to plan events, activities, parties, etc. I always had to have a picture so that I could visualize the plan. Faith for me was the road map I envisioned, and I wanted God to bless it.

My first impression up until that call from Hans was that we were just friends. I really didn't think about Hans all that much outside of the work setting. His first call threw me for a loop.

Hans and I continued to talk periodically. One day he called to tell me that the Valparaiso Boys & Girls Club was creating a new development director position that would fit me perfectly.

I remember thinking, *Really? Is this some sort of sign?*
I applied for the position and was invited for a job interview.
I heard a voice in me say, *Do it! Go and see what happens.*

So I went for the interview. I was so excited because it was something new and exciting. I had never lived outside of Minnesota.

I had talked to my dad about my plan, and he was very supportive. I truly believe he wanted to see me happy. He took me to the airport and picked me up as I traveled between Chicago and Minneapolis. Valparaiso was one hour from Midway airport, and my parents were one hour from the Minneapolis Airport.

I was offered the job, and before I could wrap my mind around how this was going to all happen, I accepted the offer.

You can say I was walking away from a life I knew into a life unseen. It wasn't easy to step out of my comfort zone. I got used to the misery and unhappiness. Despite my inner resolve to start a new life, it wasn't without its difficulties. For one thing, it was hard and a little scary to leave what was familiar: my friends, my hometown, my parents, and my sister. I had never considered moving out of Minnesota. I thought my life was in Minnesota.

And yet, faith is stepping out and believing that what lies ahead is better than what we are leaving behind. Even though I didn't have control over the situation, I was experiencing new energy and a zest for life.

I made the decision to leave my marriage, take the job, and move to Valparaiso, Indiana, not really knowing anyone but Hans and a few others at the Boys & Girls Club (BGCOPC).

As I talked over my plans with Hans, he said, "Over time, your family and friends will see how happy you are."

The time came to tell my parents that I was moving. I went to their house, sat down at the dining room table, and shared the news. My mom wanted to hear nothing of it. I then told my older sister (we were good friends), and she, too, did not like the idea. I am not sure I had any other support but my dad's.

"You know where you have been, but you don't know where you are going. You can always come back," my dad said.

In October 1998, I moved to Valparaiso, Indiana, from St. Cloud, Minnesota, to start a new life. Hans helped me find a place to live. He came to Minnesota to help me move, and another new journey began. In my heart, I knew I could not continue with what I had been doing with my life in St. Cloud.

I felt in control and confident of how I was going to live my life. I had a "do-over."

Learn to trust the journey even when you don't understand it.

Lisa leaving Minnesota

Lisa in Minnesota before leaving for Indiana

"HOLD ON TO YOUR DREAMS"

Hold on to your dreams,
Don't ever give in.
If you keep trying,
You're going to win .

Hold on to your dreams,
Though sometimes it's hard.
Just hold your head up
And reach for your stars.

Hold on to your dreams,
Though they seem far away,
And those dreams will come true,
Somehow, some way!

Hold on to your dreams.

* * *

Hans

Meeting Lisa

The first time that Lisa and I met was at a regional Boys & Girls Club conference. Both the St. Cloud Minnesota and the Porter County Indiana organizations sent many employees to the conferences. We met in Milwaukee in October of 1996 and talked in social and seminar groups. My marriage was on the rocks, and my mother's deteriorating health due to Alzheimer's left me depressed and searching for ways to cope. I was having difficulty accepting the fact that she was dying and that she could not remember who I was.

The next time that I ran into Lisa was in Indianapolis in the fall of 1997. We both were in failing marriages and loved working with children, but neither of us was going to be parents in our current situation. Lisa's husband could not have kids, and my wife did not want kids. Employees from both organizations went out to dinner with each other and networked. Lisa and I spent hours talking after dinners and found that we had a lot more in common. We talked late into the night about music, family, work, and the things we liked to do in our free time, such as camping and traveling. I was surprised when I was attracted to Lisa even though my marriage was over in my mind. When the conference ended, I thought to myself that she was a pretty amazing person and someone that I would like to see more of.

Hans at the Club

I had been living in a different part of the house that my previous wife, and I had shared until I filed for divorce and moved out in February of 1998. I tried to focus on my job by working many extra hours and keeping myself occupied.

That spring, when I was getting our men's soccer team together, a group of the guys said that their wives had told them they could still play soccer but not on my team. The team and our wives were close and did many social events together. Some of the wives had gotten together and decided that their husbands should not have any contact with me at all since they felt that I was totally to blame for our breakup.

I got some different players together, and for the next few seasons, we competed against each other. It was painful to me that I did something that I believed was absolutely the right thing to do and felt totally ostracized by it. Those days were marked by anger and frustration.

That summer a position for a development director was going to be created at the Porter County Boys & Girls Club due to the growth of the organization. I called Lisa to let her know about the job as she had told me that she would consider a move out of Minnesota if a good opportunity presented itself. She knew many of the staff in Valparaiso, and we were friends. Both of us thought that something more could develop. I knew that this was a difficult decision because family was so important to Lisa.

We Fall in Love and Get Married

Lisa

Faith makes things possible but not guaranteed easy.

I n October 1998, I moved to Valparaiso from Minnesota. With my dad's blessing, my dog Duster, and my cat Maverick, I left St. Cloud, Minnesota—which I had called home for twenty-four years. I left family, friends, and a predictable life to move over five hundred miles to Valparaiso, Indiana, for a new job, a new place to live, new friends, and the unknown. The move was certainly not something easy.

The new adventure was exciting but didn't come without me being nervous and wondering if this was the right move. I found a two-bedroom duplex that allowed me to have Duster and Maverick and was in a nice neighborhood. I had all my personal belongings and quickly made it feel like home. My move to Valparaiso was the first time I lived alone in thirty-two years. I loved being by myself, so time alone wasn't something that bothered me.

I lived only a couple of miles from my new job. Everyone at the Boys & Girls Clubs was very welcoming and made me feel at home. It first felt like a vacation with so many new things to see and do. For the first couple of months in Valparaiso, I had to deal with the finalization of my divorce. I am very thankful to my dad for taking care of these details for me and helping to bring things to a closure.

My new office was in the same building as Hans's. I worked Monday through Friday, 8:00 a.m. to 5:00 p.m. Hans worked from Tuesday to Friday, from 12:00 p.m. to 9:00 p.m., and Saturdays. Hans was very well-liked at the club and throughout the community. I really took to Hans's passion for working with kids and how he wanted to make a difference. The kids at the club really liked him, and so did the employees he supervised. Hans had a positive attitude and a quick sense of humor. He was smart, levelheaded, mature, loving, and compassionate. Just an all-around great guy.

Hans and I would mostly see each other at work since our schedules were opposite. He made it a point to introduce me to some of his friends outside the Boys & Girls Club. A couple of the lady friends would invite me out to dinner and would share with me all the details they thought I should know about Hans. Many times, their opinion was the opposite of my perception of who Hans was. I would think to myself, *Is there truth to what they are telling me? Is Hans really bullheaded and insensitive?* They would question me about the details of Hans's marriage and ask if he was divorced yet. At first it was fun to go out with these ladies, but then I started to lose interest in the information they were sharing. I felt like they were pumping me for personal information that I was not comfortable talking about and that wasn't any of their business.

Hans and I gradually started spending more time together. We turned to each other for comfort through our recent breakups, and we enjoyed each other's company. Early on in our relationship, Hans and I did a lot of fun things together. He took me to places that I had never dreamed of. I am very much a romantic, and I loved the bed-and-breakfasts we went to. We took two weeks and went on a trip up to Duluth (a place I absolutely love) around the Northern Peninsula, to Mackinac Island, down the west coast of Michigan to Ludington, where we took the SS *Badger* back to Minnesota. We went to Arkansas to visit his mom, to Hot Springs and Eureka Springs, down to Key West. My favorite trip was a seven-day Caribbean cruise. Hans also took me to several concerts, and we always had a great time. I thought, *For sure this guy is truly amazing. How did I get so lucky?*

First bed-and-breakfast

Cruise boat

Hans's friends became my friends. Getting together with them was tough at times because they were all a part of Hans's previous life with his ex. We would get together on weekends, go to concerts, have dinner at someone's home, or go out for drinks. I liked my wine, but Hans always ordered beer.

Hans's best friend's wife was best friends with his ex. The four of them took lots of trips together. One day when I was at Hans's, his best friend came over and told him he couldn't associate with him anymore because of the divorce. Being the guy Hans was, he said, "Okay." Hans wasn't going to show me how hurt he was over it.

Hans was also dealing with the stress of living far from his mom who was suffering from Alzheimer's. This was a hard time for him. He would call her once or twice a week, and there were times she didn't know him. I could hear the frustration in his voice while he tried to carry on a normal conversation. I never knew anyone who had Alzheimer's. All I could do was be supportive.

In November 1998, I started to have gastrointestinal issues. I went to several doctors, had several tests, and found out I had ulcerative colitis. I was very sick. I was on steroids, colon medication, and had several colonoscopies. I found out from my doctor that ulcerative colitis was hereditary, but both my parents were sure they didn't have it. Hans was very good to me during this time. He took me to appointments up in Chicago, made me meals, and was very comforting. He never made me feel like I was an inconvenience. Hans really would have done anything for me.

Gradually, over the next four months, Hans and I would spend more and more time together. Hans was easy to get along with. He wanted a family, and so did I, but we knew time might be against us. I also was not happy that he didn't seem to be prioritizing his divorce. His ex-wife was having a hard time and did have not have the urgency to sell the house that they owned jointly. I gave Hans an ultimatum and told him I could not continue our relationship if his divorce was not final.

In January 1999, Hans's divorce was finally concluded. He took his settlement and bought a new house in Valparaiso. It was a nice house but seemed unnecessarily large. Still, I was excited to help him decorate it.

That February on Valentine's Day, we were sitting at the island in his house having dinner, and he presented me with a box.

"I want to do life with you. Will you be my wife?"

I opened the box, and there was a beautiful diamond ring. I absolutely had no idea.

"Of course!" I said. I was the happiest I had been in years, and finally, my life was going in the right direction.

I was so excited to get married. Hans had helped get me through some rough times. I trusted him, he became my best friend, and everything seemed to be going as planned. I was exactly where I was supposed to be. We both had great jobs and a new house, and our future looked bright. I was determined to not make the same mistakes this time around.

We decided to get married July 2, 1999, because it fell on a Friday, and with it being the Fourth of July weekend, those traveling from out of town could stay through Monday. Hans and I both knew we wanted a small wedding, with just immediate family and close friends.

We booked the whole Aberdeen Bed and Breakfast in Valparaiso. The house had nine rooms, which would accommodate my family and a few of our friends. They had a gazebo that was used for outdoor weddings. Hans's best friend of twenty years was his best man, and both my sisters were my maids of honor. I wore a nontraditional ivory dress, and the rest of the wedding was very simple. Our neighbor, who was a Lutheran pastor, married us.

We wanted a wedding that was nothing like both of our first weddings. The day of the wedding, it was one hundred degrees. The guys all played golf, and the ladies relaxed and got ready for the wedding. The ceremony was beautiful, and the reception was very laid-back: buffet dinner, carrot cake, small dance, a lot of reminiscing, and fireworks. After the festive weekend, everyone went home, and we went to Door County for a relaxing four-day honeymoon. Everything was perfect—not elaborate, but very much what we wanted it to be.

Perfect couple

Lisa and her Dad

* * *

Hans

In October of 1998, Lisa was hired, and I helped her find an apartment. She did not have a lot of things, but there was no one to help her move to Valparaiso. So I, with not completely altruistic motives, offered to help. When she had moved and was settling in, I asked her out on a formal date. We started to get serious about our relationship soon after. It seemed as though all the things that we wanted from a spouse, we found in each other.

When I first got married, we did not make a decision about a family but put it on the back burner to be decided later. We went on a lot of vacations and mostly lived a hedonistic lifestyle with very little depth. As time went on, my ex-wife became more firm about not having children. Because of my coaching and working at the Boys & Girls Club, I realized that I definitely wanted a family.

During that time, my divorce was still not finalized because I had been procrastinating. I hadn't been living with my soon-to-be ex-wife, so I did not see any urgency. When Lisa and I started to get more serious, I knew that I had to get the divorce done. It was in January when it happened. I started looking for a house to buy and ended up buying a family house in a nice subdivision, which was almost the opposite of what I started looking for. A few months later, on Valentine's Day 1999, we got engaged to be married. I realized that all these things were happening quickly, but I did not question it because it all felt so right.

Shortly after I closed on the house, we took a cruise, and I thought things could not get any better. I was engaged to an awesome woman. We had good jobs, just bought a new house, and were planning a wedding. I realized that after we got married, things did not fit right with some of our friends. We noticed that one couple was very materialistic, one couple partied constantly, one couple gossiped so much that we stopped having conversations of any depth with them, and another was continuously degrading other people. Suddenly, people that were my closest friends started to have little appeal to Lisa and me.

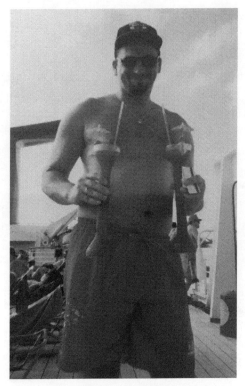

Hans on Cruise

We found a church that we liked and became friends with some of the members. Lisa was always more outgoing than I was, so I only socialized with people as couples. I was still a little nervous about how other people would view my separation, divorce, new relationship, and marriage within a couple of years even though I knew that it was the right thing to do.

The employees of the Boys & Girls Club that I worked at were supportive. After I moved out of the house, I worked a lot and went to my apartment by myself.

The members of the Boys & Girls Club that we worked at had an incredible "wedding" ceremony in the game room for us. Lisa and I were both called to the game room over the intercom, and they had the room decorated with ribbon and streamers. The club members all were guests, and one of them was the minister. They had a veil for Lisa and a top hat for me. I thought that things could not get any better, especially when we had a dream wedding on July 2, 1999.

We rented a bed-and-breakfast for the wedding party to stay at for the weekend and celebrated with a few close friends and family. Our honeymoon consisted of a trip to Door County in Wisconsin. We went hiking, sailing, shopping, going to fish boils, and visiting lighthouses. We went to one antique store with a lot of beautiful things. Lisa and I love nautical decor. Walking around a corner at the shop, we saw hanging on the wall a piece of slate about the size of a license plate. It was painted with a sailboat and a lighthouse, and it said, "The Schellers." We took it to the checkout in order to buy it, and the owner said that they could put our name on another one for us. We told them we would like that one because that was our name. It turned out that it was the shop owners' names also, even though they were not related to us.

It was a perfect start to married life.

Hans and Lisa's wedding

Starting a Family

Lisa

Hans and I Wanted to Start a Family Immediately

Faith is trusting the unseen.

I n September 1999, my dream came true. I was pregnant. This was amazing! God was so good. The first five months of the pregnancy were good, but I had a lot of morning sickness. Then at about six months, I was diagnosed with high blood pressure. I couldn't believe it. The doctors had to keep a close eye on the pregnancy. It became a high-risk pregnancy. I was placed on bed rest and needed to go to the hospital for blood pressure readings three times a week. Hans was a very attentive husband and really took care of me. He bought a bell for me to ring if I needed anything, and many friends brought over meals.

On April 29, at thirty-four weeks, my doctor decided I needed to be induced because the baby was not growing as expected. We were not one-hundred-percent sure I was having a girl. I truly trusted and had faith in my doctor that she would bring us through it. I was admitted to the hospital and hooked up to Pitocin and steroids; they were not sure about the lung development of the baby.

After eighteen hours in labor, Hannah Hilde was born at four pounds and one ounce on April 30, 2000, six weeks early. Hilde is the name of Hans's mom, and we thought it would be special to give Hannah her name. I didn't get to see Hannah right away because she was whisked off to NICU and hooked up to IVs. For many, having a baby in the NICU would be very frightening, as I had thought it would be, but I knew from the doctor that Hannah would probably be in better hands in the real world than in my body. At this point, it was my body fighting the baby for nutrients. I finally had my little girl. I remember telling my grandma that someday I was going to have a little girl, and her name was going to be Hannah. Hannah came into this world as a fighter—very determined and strong-willed. My dreams were coming true. Hans was an amazing husband, and I knew he was going to be an awesome daddy.

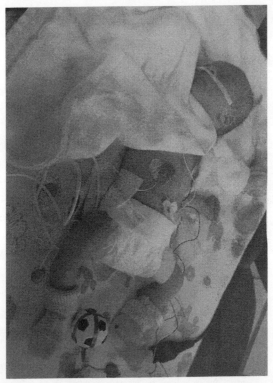

Hannah, NICU

While in the hospital, Hans and I met a couple in NICU. There was a lady who just had a baby boy, and he also was in the NICU. She was the first person to see Hannah as she was rushed into the room and hooked up to wires while having a needle put in her head. Everything was a blur after Hannah's birth. The doctors shared with us the risks of having a preemie baby and the developmental delays she might have. It was a scary and stressful time because neither Hans nor I had known anyone who had dealt with a baby in NICU. I didn't have family nearby for support, and we relied heavily on our friends as well as each other. Hans and I were not active churchgoers, so we didn't have a church family, but I know we had many people praying for us. I also believed in my heart that God was always going to take care of us and he would never leave us. My new friend and I supported each other during the ten days while our babies were in the hospital. When it was time for all of us to go home, we exchanged telephone numbers and agreed to stay in touch. Little did I know of the friendship God had planned for us!

I loved being a mom and a wife to Hans.

One hundred years from now, it will not matter what kind of car we drove, what kind of house we lived in, not how much money we made, but the world will be better because of the lives we raised.

Bringing Hannah home

Lisa's mom and Hannah

In September 2000, Hans and I thought it would be in our best interest to put our house up for sale and move to Minnesota to be closer to my family so that Hannah would grow up around extended family. Our house was not sold, but we thought we could leave half our stuff in Valparaiso and bring half to Minnesota. My brother had a lake house near Mankato that he said we could live in. Our thoughts were to move and get jobs. Then, once the house sold, we could find a house.

So once again, this time with Hans and Hannah, we packed up the U-Haul with what we thought we needed and headed to Minnesota. I was excited to move back to Minnesota because I knew where we were going and it was familiar to me. Hans, on the other hand, was leaving Valparaiso, Indiana, where he lived for thirty-six years—leaving family, friends, and all of what he knew—to start a new life in Minnesota. Hans had met my brother once and the rest of my family a handful of times. Hans was looking forward to a fresh beginning. He told me he would be happy anywhere Hannah and I were.

We left Valparaiso in October 2000, and as we drove into the driveway at my brother's, Hans received a call that his mom had passed away after a long battle with Alzheimer's. Hans and I had a trip to Key West planned the next week after our move. He got on a plane and headed to Arkansas, and I went to my parents to drop off Hannah before meeting back up with Hans in Florida. Again, it was a whirlwind of an adventure. A move back to Minnesota, a new place to live, new jobs, and a new baby. Hans and I were determined that as long as we were together, we were going to be fine.

Key West

After our trip to Florida, we came back to our new home near Mankato on German Lake. We settled in the best we could.

Hans got a job at the post office, and I worked for my brother since I could bring Hannah to work with me. Those three months we were there felt like an eternity. The winter was awful. When we went back to Valparaiso to check on our house during December, we asked ourselves, "What are we doing?" Moving to Minnesota was much harder than we thought it was going to be. Jobs weren't better. Living arrangements were not better. The weather was not better, and we did not see my family any more than we did before except for my brother and his family.

It wasn't easy telling my family we were heading back to Valparaiso, Indiana, but with the help of my sister and brother-in-law, we packed up the U-Haul again and brought everything back to the place we called home.

After our December visit to Valparaiso, we decided that we should move back to our nice house once again and find jobs that would suit us. So in February 2001, we moved back to Valparaiso. Hans went back to work for the Boys & Girls Club, and I started Gift Baskets Galore.

Having my own business was an exciting new adventure for me. I knew I wanted to have a professional career and the flexibility to take care of Hannah. How fun would it be to have my own business? I thought of a gift basket business. I was creative and enjoyed working with people, and I could balance it all. My original plan was to run the business from home, make baskets, and sell to companies. We took some of our retirement money and took a leap of faith. Hans thought I needed to have a storefront for the business. I wasn't one-hundred-percent sold on the idea, but we found a commercial place in downtown Valparaiso that was reasonable, and on Lincolnway, we opened Gift Baskets Galore in March of 2001.

The walk-in business was slow, and the overhead was high. It was in August that the retail businesses started to stock up for the holidays. Hans and I knew it was going to take a little investing to see the return. I ordered holiday supplies, rented additional space from the landlord for the basket-making prep and storing supplies, advertised for the holidays, and hoped it was going to be a great season. Then September 11 happened, and no one knew how this was going to affect the economy.

Hans and I took a vacation to Florida in early October, came back ready for a busy holiday season, and nothing. The economy was slow. No one was buying extras.

Bed and Breakfast Key West, Florida

During this time, we tried day care for Hannah, and it didn't work. She got the typical ear infections and other bugs you get at day care. I talked with my friend whom I had met at the hospital, and she, too, was looking for day care. We decided to hire someone together to watch the kids. A couple of days a week, the kids would be at our house, and then on Fridays, Hannah would go to Hans's aunt. Hans's aunt was the closest to Oma on his side of the family. Hannah loved going there. I would usually pick up Hannah at 5:00 p.m., around the time Hans's uncle came home. I would stay and visit for a while. We would talk at the table, and Hans's uncle would have a few beers and shots while his aunt had her drink. I did not drink. I knew this kind of socializing was a culture for the Germans. Family gatherings with Hans's side of the family were very typical German gatherings. It was not unusual for Hans to drink beer; it was what Germans did.

Oma and Hannah

It was April 2001, and I remember having to be in the garage to get something. I opened this locker that belonged to Hans, and inside there were five or six bottles of vodka. I was in disbelief, but I attributed it to him being stressed because of all the changes. I had seen Hans drink beer but never hard alcohol. I called my older sister, told her about the alcohol, and we both seemed a little confused, but I didn't really think much about it. I never mentioned it to Hans. I was so preoccupied with balancing the business, the house chores, and Hannah that it didn't seem to affect me.

The economy had slowed down, and so did the business. No one knew what the future held.

Hannah and Lisa, the day Lisa found alcohol bottles in the garage cabinet

In November 2001, I found out I was pregnant again. After having Hannah, my doctors had said, "You aren't doing this again," and I had said, "No, Hannah is not going to be an only child."

I was ecstatic once again! Finally, all my dreams were coming true. I was about four months into my pregnancy when I started to bleed. I went to see my doctor, and she did an ultrasound. I was pregnant with fraternal twins, and one of the twins did not make it. I always thought it would be a real blessing to have twins, but that was not in the plans.

Once again, I had a high-risk pregnancy. Not knowing the sex of the babies, I was told that if the living baby was a male and he recognized the other baby was gone, I might lose the other baby as well. Further into my pregnancy, I developed high blood pressure and was placed on bed rest.

It was July 13, and I had just been to the hospital for a blood pressure reading. We came home and went on a little walk. Then my water broke. We called our friends to pick up Hannah, and off we went to the hospital. Still not knowing the sex, I thought, *For sure this one is a boy.* But to our surprise, it was a baby girl.

We didn't really have a name picked out, so Hans offered the name Delaney. I thought, *Wow, that is a beautiful name.* On July 14, we welcomed Delaney Ann at five pounds and seven ounces. Delaney was four weeks early. Her middle name, Ann, came from my mom, Shirley Ann. When I called my mom to tell her, she was in disbelief. She said, "You named her after me?" From there, her name was not just Delaney to my mom but Delaney Ann.

Delaney Ann as a newborn

A little while later, I went to the Chamber of Commerce to become a member. There was a guy there who asked if my business was a woman-owned business. I said yes, and he mentioned there were opportunities for me to work with larger corporations that were required to work with minority businesses. I filled out the paperwork and became eligible to promote my business to companies such as casinos. I got my first call from what was Harrah's Casino in East Chicago at the time. I went to the meeting, and they hired me to make gourmet food and bath baskets for the casino and player development items for special events.

The business was booming just from this opportunity. I decided I didn't need a storefront with the overhead to provide services to the casino. They were not coming to my business—I was going to them. At the end of 2001, we decided to close the storefront. We had a couple of months on our lease left, but it wasn't worth all the extra labor and bills to keep it open. Ninety percent of the money went toward expenses at the storefront, and 10 percent of the income was from the walk-in business. We moved the business to our basement. It became very lucrative. We were now in business with three casinos and started an additional entity called Community Connections, which provided baskets for new homeowners featuring logos and advertising items from local businesses—a similar concept to the Welcome Wagon. Before we knew it, our business flourished.

Gift Baskets Galore Entrepreneur Award

Meanwhile, Hans went back to working for the Boys & Girls Club as well as was refinishing furniture on the side. We had a lot going on, and we were trying to balance it all. As the small gift basket business grew, it was profiting more than we could imagine. We needed to either hire someone or have Hans quit the Boys & Girls Club so that he could take over the sales for Community Connection, deliver the baskets, and help our business grow even more. After weighing the pros and cons, that was what we decided. Again, another leap of faith.

Hans quit his job, and we started to work more side by side. I was the basket maker and the financial manager, and Hans was the sales and delivery person. Before we knew it, we started to outgrow our basement and needed more space. We could either rent space again or build a larger house and dedicate the entire basement to the business. I always had ideas after ideas, and Hans always seemed to go along with them.

Now my life was complete. I was married to my best friend. I had a nice home, two beautiful daughters, a successful business, great friends, and a wonderful family. I was living life my way, and things were going really well. I was very happy.

After the girls were born, I tried to be the perfect mother, have a successful career, and be an awesome wife . . .

Birthdays and holidays were always celebrated with lots of decorations, presents, family, friends, food, and drinks.

There were lots of playdates for the girls. I got them involved in kinder music, yoga, dance, art, gymnastics, soccer, T-ball, theater, etc. I was going to give them the opportunity to participate in it all.

Both girls had attended Montessori school since they were eighteen months old. I always made sure their clothes were ironed, their hair was perfect, and their lunches were nutritious. We all dressed the part.

Church as well was a priority in our lives. I wanted to make sure the girls were raised in a Christian home. The girls attended Sunday school and vacation Bible school during the summer. I taught Sunday school. Hans ushered, and we were involved in friendship groups. We loved our Lutheran church and made great Christian friends. Hans enjoyed socializing because he knew a lot of people from being in the community for so long.

We had a huge circle of friends. Every weekend there was something to look forward to.

* * *

Hans

I resigned from the Boys & Girls Club to pursue refinishing furniture on a full-time basis after having done both for the entire summer of 1999. That fall we discovered that we were pregnant, and Lisa was having a very difficult pregnancy, so I tried to be a loving, supportive husband, especially when she was forced to be on bed rest in the last trimester. I even bought her a small bell that she could ring if she needed me. It also allowed me to spend a lot of time in the garage, working and drinking . . .

Hannah Hilde was brought into this world on April 30, 2000, at four pounds and one ounce and six weeks early. She was rushed off to the neonatal intensive care unit, where she would fall under four pounds before stabilizing. She changed our whole lives. The nursery at a hospital is an emotional and joyous place.

The first time that I went into the NICU, I was nervous and passed beds where two-pound babies lay and others had a dozen needles in them. It was a much more somber place. I spotted Hannah's crib right away because on a railing, tied with a green ribbon, was a miniature soccer ball. I did not know who could have put it there or even had access to the room. I later found out that it was Dr. Alice Harrington, who was a pediatrician in Valpo. We knew each other through the Boys & Girls Club, and she was aware of my love for soccer and was thoughtful enough to place it on Hannah's crib.

Hannah seemed so fragile. She had a needle in her scalp because there was no other vein that the doctors could find. Hannah's nickname Bug came from the fact that she was jaundiced and had to lie on a pad that glowed green, and she looked like a lightning bug when she lay on it. In the NICU there was a baby boy in the bed next to Hannah named Robbie. They were born a couple of days apart. We got to know the family and ended up becoming friends. On top of all the major life changes going on, we decided to embark on yet another adventure. Family has always been important to us, and with my mom suffering from Alzheimer's, we decided to move closer to Lisa's family in Minnesota.

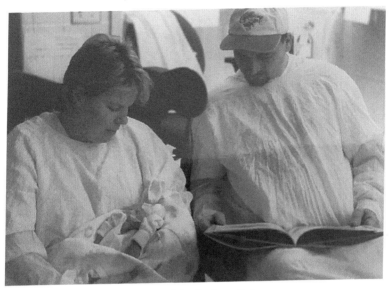

Hannah in the hospital

We put our house on the market, rounded up some friends to help, and moved in October 2000 to a remote lake cabin where Lisa's brother let us stay at. I quit the refinishing business I had started, with only a part-time job at a local post office lined up, and also tried to start a new refinishing business in Minnesota. An incredibly brutal winter followed. We had a thirty-minute drive to the nearest town on a clear day and were snowbound for quite a few days. We did not make any money when we couldn't work and had an infant to take care of, so the pressure was building, which led to more and more stress.

While we were moving, my mother's Alzheimer's started to worsen. We got the call the first day that we were in Minnesota that I should go to her because she might not make it another day. I immediately got on a flight. My mother was a saint with the most positive outlook on life imaginable. One of her favorite sayings about her disease was, "This isn't too bad—now I forget to smoke cigarettes," with a big smile on her face.

Hans's mom in Arkansas

When my mom passed away on October 30, 2000, she was sixty-two years old. She had been diagnosed when she was fifty-six. I saw her waste away both physically and mentally without really anything that could be done about it.

After her funeral, my mother's boyfriend informed us that she had changed her will and had given him the house and all the property, which was a huge shock to us because my mom was all about family and had spoken to us many times about whether my brother or I would live in the house after she passed away. He showed us a new will that had recently been drafted with a signature that did not look like my mother's precise handwriting.

Later that day, while my brother took me to the airport, we talked about what to do about the altering of the will. I hired an attorney in Arkansas, who assured us that we would prevail, and because of my mother's mental state at the time of the new will, it would be declared null and void. After about two years of continuances, depositions, and expert statements, a judge found that the new will would stand and we would not receive anything from the will. I am sure that the fact that the judge was a friend of my mom's boyfriend might have had something to do with the verdict, and being an outsider from eight hundred miles away did not help either. All this completely contradicted my mom's feelings on family and her hope that my brother and I would share the house someday.

The boyfriend told me that he would ship her cremated remains and some photos to me. I was crushed when I received a box that had a few pictures with broken frames and a large ziplock bag with her ashes in them. I believed in my heart that what he did was defiling the memory of my mom and her wishes and that he knew it. I felt that he was purposely doing this to *me* and not my mom. I was taking it personally, and I was mad. My anger was taken out on all the people around me and not the person whom I blamed for it all. It took me many years to realize that the most important thing was that my mom was able to spend the last years of her life at home, being taken care of. That truly was the only thing that mattered, but I didn't see it. Actually, I did see it, but I just did not put it into proper perspective. The house, the land, and the change in the will were minuscule compared to that. My brother never seemed to grasp that and started spiraling deeper into his own addiction.

Lisa and I had a vacation to Florida planned at that time, so when I flew to Arkansas for the funeral, Lisa flew to Key West. I got on a flight to join Lisa in Florida, but not before buying a small bottle of orange juice and a large bottle of vodka just to tide me over on the trip. The trip to Key West was about as enjoyable as it could be, considering the circumstances. In hindsight, my mother's death affected me more than I thought because the wound was deep and not always visible. I had a hard time believing in a God who could take away a woman who was so loving and caring and let other people who were hateful live long, healthy lives. I did not understand for a long time that there is a reason for everything but it may not be understood at the time.

The house had not sold yet, so during Christmas, we decided to go back to Valparaiso to check on the house. We slept on a mattress on the floor of the living room in front of the fireplace and contemplated what we had done and where to go from there. After a lot of soul-searching, we decided to move back later that winter and salvage what we could back in Indiana. So many things had happened to us in a short time that we did not really know which way to turn. But honestly, the really bad times were just starting.

Whoever fights monsters should see to it that in the process he does not become a monster. And if you gaze long enough into an abyss, the abyss will gaze back at you.

—*Friedrich Nietzsche*

In March of 2001, Lisa started a gift basket business, and I tried to resume my refinishing business. I tried to work in the garage, but it was cold, dusty, and not a good place to work. My daily drinking had started. One evening Lisa needed something in the garage and opened a locker to get it but was met with an avalanche of empty liquor bottles that I had stashed. Secretly, I was glad she had opened the locker with the empty bottles instead of the next locker with all the full ones. I tried to explain that I was drinking more and hiding it to relieve stress and did not want her to worry about it. I had not even considered that I was an alcoholic. I always joked that I couldn't be one because I just drank; alcoholics went to meetings. It seemed like every social event I went to or hosted involved alcohol. By the fall of 2001, I was a full-blown alcoholic. I could not handle life's daily pressures and had to escape.

In November of 2001, we found out that Lisa was pregnant again and prayed that there would be no complications. Shortly thereafter, an ultrasound showed that she was going to have twins. In February, the doctor informed us that Lisa was only pregnant with one child and the other was a "disappearing twin." It was another trip on our emotional roller coaster that I tried to level out with alcohol.

On the Fourth of July in 2002, Lisa and I were with our friends at the beach. Both Lisa and her friend were in their last month of pregnancy, and her friend started to go into labor. We hustled back to their house, and they went to the hospital. That evening their second son Jack was born, and ten days later, on July 14, 2002, our second daughter, Delaney, was born. Our family was complete.

Lisa developed a type of Welcome Wagon basket for new residents in Porter County as part of her gift basket business that took off. It was called Community Connections. I was working back at the Boys & Girls Club in the same position I had held about ten years prior and started to do some furniture refinishing in the garage again. Community Connections started to take off, and I ended up leaving the Boys & Girls club again in order to help Lisa and do my refinishing.

A couple of years after Delaney was born, we decided to do our first real family trip—one week at Disney in Orlando. We were all excited, especially the girls. We got great pictures and memories and managed to get to most of the different parks. Our Cross Creek house gave us many friends, including some who are still friends today. This happened in February right after we bought the land and had started to build our new home.

Delaney coming home from the hospital

Upbringing

Lisa

I was born in Grand Rapids, Minnesota, in 1965. I am the second of four children. My older sister is seventeen months older than me, my brother is thirteen months younger, and my younger sister is two and a half years younger than me. We lived in Floodwood until I was two years old and then St. Paul until I was five or six. The next move was to a small rural town, St. Joseph, Minnesota, where we lived in the country in a community called Pleasant Acres. It was a development of maybe one hundred homes on one of Minnesota's ten thousand lakes.

Our family loved living in Pleasant Acres. There was so much to do and so many families with children our ages. The community had a park with tennis courts, basketball courts, horseshoes, barbecue stations, and lake access. In the summertime, we would fish and go boating. My dad taught swimming lessons to all the children in the neighborhood. We would play and make forts in the woods, ride our bikes for hours, and so much more. In the winter months, we ice-skated and went sledding, and the biggest highlight was taking out the snowmobiles. My dad would hook up the toboggan to the snowmobiles, and he would take us kids out going up and down the ditches. We had so much fun. Family vacations, such as camping and traveling, were always so much fun. My parents also liked to be involved in the community. There were neighborhood parties, family snowmobile trips, as well as Halloween and Christmas parties. I did a lot of babysitting for the families in the neighborhood.

Two-month-old Lisa with her older sister, Sheila

My dad was a high school teacher, athletic director, coach, driver education teacher, financial planner, and entrepreneur. My mom held many different jobs—from being an Avon lady to being a self-taught painter, as well as being an executive director of a YWCA. My parents did whatever they needed to do to raise four children. They were not afraid to try new things and take on opportunities.

My dad was an athletic director, coach, and teacher at Cathedral High School. My parents chaperoned high school outings to New York and Washington, DC, and ski trips in which we kids went along. We had a lot of great memories in St. Joseph. While chaperoning a ski trip to Grand Marais, Minnesota, my mom broke her leg in seven places. She was in the hospital in Grand Marais for a week. Then when she came home, they had to rebreak her leg and reset it. She was in a wheelchair, full cast, and then half a cast for nine months. The four of us kids needed to pick up responsibilities very quickly at a young age. I became the caretaker. This was a hard time for my mom because she needed to count on other people, which was not her. My mom was active about ten years prior and started to do some furniture refinishing in the garage again. Community Connections started to take off, and I ended up leaving the Boys & Girls club again in order to help Lisa and do my refinishing.

A couple of years after Delaney was born, we decided to do our first real family trip—one week at Disney in Orlando. We were all excited, especially the girls. We got great pictures and memories and managed to get to most of the different parks. Our Cross Creek house gave us many friends, including some who are still friends today. This happened in February right after we bought the land and had started to build our new home.

Delaney coming home from the hospital

Upbringing

Lisa

I was born in Grand Rapids, Minnesota, in 1965. I am the second of four children. My older sister is seventeen months older than me, my brother is thirteen months younger, and my younger sister is two and a half years younger than me. We lived in Floodwood until I was two years old and then St. Paul until I was five or six. The next move was to a small rural town, St. Joseph, Minnesota, where we lived in the country in a community called Pleasant Acres. It was a development of maybe one hundred homes on one of Minnesota's ten thousand lakes.

Our family loved living in Pleasant Acres. There was so much to do and so many families with children our ages. The community had a park with tennis courts, basketball courts, horseshoes, barbecue stations, and lake access. In the summertime, we would fish and go boating. My dad taught swimming lessons to all the children in the neighborhood. We would play and make forts in the woods, ride our bikes for hours, and so much more. In the winter months, we ice-skated and went sledding, and the biggest highlight was taking out the snowmobiles. My dad would hook up the toboggan to the snowmobiles, and he would take us kids out going up and down the ditches. We had so much fun. Family vacations, such as camping and traveling, were always so much fun. My parents also liked to be involved in the community. There were neighborhood parties, family snowmobile trips, as well as Halloween and Christmas parties. I did a lot of babysitting for the families in the neighborhood.

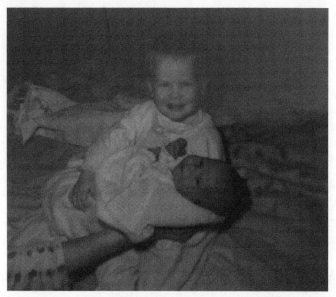

Two-month-old Lisa with her older sister, Sheila

My dad was a high school teacher, athletic director, coach, driver education teacher, financial planner, and entrepreneur. My mom held many different jobs—from being an Avon lady to being a self-taught painter, as well as being an executive director of a YWCA. My parents did whatever they needed to do to raise four children. They were not afraid to try new things and take on opportunities.

My dad was an athletic director, coach, and teacher at Cathedral High School. My parents chaperoned high school outings to New York and Washington, DC, and ski trips in which we kids went along. We had a lot of great memories in St. Joseph. While chaperoning a ski trip to Grand Marais, Minnesota, my mom broke her leg in seven places. She was in the hospital in Grand Marais for a week. Then when she came home, they had to rebreak her leg and reset it. She was in a wheelchair, full cast, and then half a cast for nine months. The four of us kids needed to pick up responsibilities very quickly at a young age. I became the caretaker. This was a hard time for my mom because she needed to count on other people, which was not her. My mom was active and enjoyed gardening, being outside, exercising, etc. At this time, my mom taught herself to paint.

Lisa and her dad

She learned tole painting and rosemaling. She went on to have a studio and teach classes to others. Her accident turned into a career that she'd prepared for herself for ten to fifteen years.

My dad was raised on a dairy farm in Taylors Falls, Minnesota, and had one older brother. Taylors Falls is located on the St. Croix River, which divides Wisconsin and Minnesota. My grandpa was from Sweden. My grandparents were married for over fifty-five years and lived well into their eighties. I was always amazed at how hard they both worked on the farm, and there seemed to be very little arguing. My grandma had beautiful huge vegetable gardens. My grandpa had well over eighty cows, and they milked them twice a day. I loved my visits to the Olson Farm. Christmas was my favorite time of the year to visit. All the snow, lights, Grandma's Christmas tree, baking, and a wonderful holiday meal. It was the only time of the year that both our family and my uncle's family would be under one roof. There were so many traditions and wonderful memories.

As I look back, I realize that my grandparents had a unique relationship. My grandpa was very quiet but very hardworking, and my grandma was strong and made a lot of the family decisions. My grandma was the oldest of seven children, and I am sure she took on a leadership role very quickly among her siblings, which carried over to her relationship with my grandpa. My grandma was in charge. My dad was maybe three and a half pounds when he was born, and eighty years ago, they had to live on prayers and faith that babies would make it as preemies. My dad had a close relationship with both his parents, but mostly his mom. He loved visiting my grandparents and the farm as often as he could.

Lisa and her Grandparents Olson

My mom, on the other hand, was born on the Iron Range in Northern Minnesota and was taken from her natural family when she was three years old due to her natural mother not being able to take care of both her brother and her. My mom was placed in and out of foster care and lived in an orphanage until she was nine, when my grandparents adopted her. My grandparents had one natural daughter, and when they found out they were not able to have additional children, the decision was made to adopt a daughter. While growing up, I thought how awful that would have been to live from home to home with no stability. It was so loving of my grandparents to adopt my mom. It wasn't what anyone expected, but they made the best of it.

My mom was raised on a poultry farm in Elbow Lake, Minnesota. Our family would see my grandparents about six times a year. We would go to my grandparents' farm, and they would come visit us. All the visits seemed to be pleasant, but you could tell there was tension. My mom didn't have as close of a relationship with my grandma as she did with my grandpa. We didn't know much about the adoption other than what we overheard. We knew my grandma was very controlling and had some mental health issues, and my mom was a lot more challenging of a child to raise than my grandma had ever expected.

My parents were married for forty-five years. My mom was eighteen and my dad was twenty-two when they married. We were brought up in the Lutheran Church, went to church on a regular basis, were baptized, made our first Communion, and were confirmed. Church was important to my parents. All of us children went to college, graduated, got a good job, and married right out of college. My parents taught us that we don't share our problems with others and we take care of them ourselves and within our family. My parents seemed to be successful. There wasn't addiction in my family (at least it wasn't mentioned) or divorce. They had good jobs and were a happy, loving couple. They were the model of a good marriage and raising a family.

Lisa's mom and dad

Lisa's family in Pleasant Acres

In 1975, I was about ten, going into fifth grade, and my parents decided to move to St. Cloud, Minnesota, which was twenty minutes from St. Joseph. My dad taught at Cathedral High School (CHS). We went to Bethlehem Lutheran Church, which was also in St. Cloud, and the school district boundaries started to change. We kids would have to take the school bus for an hour one way to and from school. The move only made sense.

I wasn't excited about the move because I loved Pleasant Acres. It was so much fun. My life wasn't going to be the same. My parents bought a nice house that was on the north side of St. Cloud, only two miles to Cathedral and five miles to the church we attended. The house was in town, which had neighborhood blocks and alleys instead of woods or lakes. This was definitely something to get used to. The house also had two efficiency apartments on the back for added income for my parents. All of us kids got our own bedroom, and mine had a bathroom.

I was also going to attend a new school, Sts. Peter and Paul Middle School, which was a parochial school. This meant Catholic, and it didn't make sense to me because we were Lutheran (but my dad did teach at Cathedral, which was Catholic). However, my parents were done with the public schools, and they wanted us to get a better education. At the public schools, I did not get very good grades.

Along with having to attend a new school (in which I needed to meet new friends and being non-Catholic), I got glasses for the first time. My self-esteem was zero. I was an awkward, four-eyed ten-year-old who was not good at school and with no friends. How was I going to survive? Of course, life went on, and I attended St. Paul's fifth grade through eighth grade.

There were only thirty-five to forty students who graduated from eighth grade with me. I eventually made friends and had two best friends. We did everything together. There were probably about fifteen friends who hung out together, both boys and girls. It was typical awkward middle school years where we were all trying to figure out where we fit in. I played volleyball and softball, and I had a paper route. We had our eighth-grade graduation, and everyone was excited to leave St. Paul's and move on to Cathedral High School or Apollo High School. Apollo was the public high school that I knew I would not be attending even if I wanted to.

During the summers, I loved spending a week at my grandparents' (my dad's parents') dairy farm in Taylors Falls. We milked cows, played in the barn, jumped in hay bales, picked rocks, cooked, and baked. I did this every summer for as long as I could remember. I had a great relationship with my grandma. She had so much wisdom, and we would have long talks about life. My grandma was very strong and courageous. She loved God, and I learned a lot from her. She taught me to quilt, needlepoint, knit, and sew. I have carried all those hobbies with me through today. My relationship with my grandma continued through college until she passed. I would always make it a point to visit her and call her regularly. Every time I visited, she made my favorite meal—fried chicken, real mashed potatoes, and peas.

Lisa's Grandma and Grandpa Olson Farm

During my high school years, I played a little volleyball and softball, but I wasn't good enough to play varsity sports. I hung out with a group of twenty-one friends, which were all a mix of guys and girls. We would go to football, basketball, and baseball games. We would also attend school dances, and I was on the yearbook committee. During this time, my friends and I experienced alcohol and cigarettes a little. Many of my friends had older brothers and sisters who could buy for us. I had a lot more guy friends than girlfriends. I couldn't stand their cattiness, gossip, and backstabbing. I tried to have friends from all walks of life. I had my friends at school. I had a really good friend with whom I went to confirmation classes. She lived around the corner, so we did things together. I had my friends from Perkins Restaurant, and I had adult friends that I babysat for.

Not only did my parents have this idea that all of us kids would work at Perkins when we turned sixteen, but also we all were going to go to Europe between our junior and senior years of high school with our French teacher, Sister Michaela. After three years of French in high school, we were eligible to go for two and a half weeks.

My European vacation was in the summer of 1982. It was quite a memorable experience. There were a dozen students from CHS and one student from another local high school, and we met up with another group. We went to Germany, Switzerland, Austria, London, and France. We took a tour bus, and I saw sights that were fascinating and beautiful—from cathedrals and castles to the Swiss mountains, Eiffel Tower, and Big Ben. We also witnessed London's changing of the guards and so much more.

One of the first places we experienced in Germany was the Hofbräuhaus in Munich. Here is where you sit at picnic-like tables while the waitresses bring out huge mugs of beer. Since Europe does not have a drinking age, Sister Michaela allowed us to have one mug of beer each, not knowing that the beer in Germany is stronger than the United States. One was enough for all of us. As the trip continued, we were able to drink in moderation. I had such an amazing time on this trip and came back to the States with my eyes a little more opened.

Family is like branches on a tree. We all grow in
different directions, yet our roots remain the same.

My senior year of high school was spent enjoying my friends, applying for colleges, etc. Life seemed normal.

I had a wonderful relationship with my dad growing up. He was always there for our family. He was understanding and patient, and he made us feel like we were always a priority. It didn't matter what was going on in our lives; he never questioned and was always supportive. I never saw my dad angry. He took life as it came and loved adventures, always trying new things. He was very empathetic and compassionate.

My mom and my relationship, on the other hand, was tough. My mom was strong and assertive. I was sensitive and quiet. My mom didn't seem to have a lot of compassion and empathy. When I was hurt, she didn't know how to comfort me. I was very emotional and sensitive. My mom seemed to always be in control and made sure we knew it. She was very strong-willed, and you didn't want to cross her. The other side of my mom was, she was very talented, artistic, and creative. She knew what she wanted, was determined, and would go for everything she put her mind to. She, too, loved adventure and new things. I always thought my dad was a saint for putting up with all he did with her, and he was. He loved my mom a lot and wanted her to be happy. There was nothing my dad wouldn't have done for her.

My dad knew my mom and her challenges. He picked up the pieces in our family. When my mom got upset with me, he would say things like, "Turn the other cheek . . ." "Don't engage in a confrontation..." "It's not worth the fight..." "Pick your battles..." My dad always supported my mom. It was like he enabled the negative. Though he might not have always agreed with her, he would find excuses for her behavior. He was the peacemaker. When we were young, I was taught to obey my parents, honor my mother and father as it is the fourth commandment, and not make waves. As I got into my teens and older, more and more distance seeped in between my mom and me. I disagreed a lot with her and started to build resentment.

Lisa's high school graduation

When it came time to decide where to go for college in 1983, I knew I did not want to go to St. Cloud State. I had a good friend who got a scholarship for volleyball at Mankato State University in Southern Minnesota, and I applied there. My friend went down to MSU a few months before school started, and she got a feel for what college life was going to be like. She called me and told me all about the Viking Training Camp, the football players, and the big campus life we were about to embark on. In my life up to the age of eighteen, I only knew one African American and no other person from another culture. Attending MSU was a culture shock. How was I going to survive all the changes?

My parents dropped me off at my new home, the dorm. Because I registered late, I was put in a transfer dorm. This was for students who were transferring from another college. I did not know my roommate. She was two years older than me and set in her ways. We were very different. She was into her studies, liked it quiet, spent a lot of time in the dorm room, and was not very social. She outgrew the stage I was in and tried to mother me. I, on the other hand, was very social. I loved going out with my friends, having a good time, and my grades were okay. After the first semester, I put in for a room change. I was able to move to the Twin Tower dorms. This was where everyone wanted to live.

Occasionally, my friend and I would end up at the same parties. She introduced me to the next guy I would have a relationship with. He was a football player, and we had a lot of the same friends. I met a guy at the end of my freshman year. I really liked him, but being at the end of my freshman year, I was going back to St. Cloud for the summer, and he was going back home, which was in Southern Minnesota. I didn't want a long-distance relationship.

In my sophomore year, I lived in the dorms, and I had a roommate who had all kinds of issues. This was the first time I experienced someone who was anorexic and bulimic, who binge-drank, and who was very OCD. We didn't really hang out together either because she was always with her boyfriend or doing her own thing. It was after Christmas, and the girl got worse with her bulimia. She had to be admitted to a rehab hospital. She was gone for six weeks and tried to come back, but it didn't work out. This was quite the experience for me. I really couldn't wrap my mind around all her issues.

In my junior year of college, I lived with four other girls in a two-bedroom apartment. Three of us were in one room and two in the other. All my roommates had boyfriends, and there were always people coming and going. Because they had boyfriends, it seemed like there were only two of us in the apartment at a time.

In the first couple of years of college, I just took my general classes. I didn't have any idea as to what I was going to major in. I met so many people, went to parties, and loved homecoming weekend. It was time to declare a major to graduate. My parents were adamant that I get a college degree, and I wasn't so sure. I did not do well in school. I finally declared a major in social work.

While I was in college, I got away from going to church. I worked every Sunday, and I didn't have a church nearby to go to. Let's just say that church wasn't a priority.

I did a work-study in the student union. I sold the tickets for the weekend movies, and I met a guy who ran the projectors. This guy and I became friends as we were spending every weekend together there. We eventually started dating. This new friend was from a German family and the youngest of five boys. We had a lot in common, and he was very good to me. I loved him, and he loved me.

I graduated in the summer of 1987 with a bachelor's degree in social work. After graduating, I put out lots of résumés. I got interviewed at adolescent rehab centers and other agencies but with no luck for a job in my field. My intentions were not to move back to St. Cloud. I never wanted to return there. I was ready for a whole new beginning.

During this time, my dad was with IDS—which is now known as Ameriprise Financial—and he was ready for change. He was offered a district manager job in Minot, North Dakota. My parents put their house in St. Cloud on the market. My younger sister had graduated from high school, and this was a time for them to take on a new adventure. My dad moved to Minot while Mom stayed to sell the house. The house did not sell, and they found a house in Minot they really liked. Well, since I had graduated from college and my older sister was in St. Cloud working at Perkins Restaurant as a manager, why don't the both of us move into the house and pay rent to cover the house payment? So we did.

I continued to look for a career job because I was determined that I was not going to be a full-time waitress with a college degree. I finally got the degree I never thought I was going to get. In August 1989, I applied at the Boys & Girls Club of Central Minnesota and was hired the next month as a site manager at KIDSTOP. Working with children was my passion. Sometimes I wish I had gotten my degree in education.

In November 1989, I got married to my college boyfriend. We married in the Lutheran church I attended as a child.

Finally, my life was moving in the right direction. I had a college degree, finally got a job related to my major, and was married to the love of my life. We found a small starter home to rent to own. I had my job at the BGC, and my husband found a job with a company like UPS called Spee-Dee Delivery. Now, after the jobs and the house, it was time to start a family. Well, that didn't come so easy.

After months of trying, we went to see a specialist, had tests run, and found out we could not have children naturally. Our journey of infertility began. We did a year of IUI treatments and three attempts of IVF that came with a whole lot of emotional stress, hormone craziness, and financial debit. But I was determined I was going to have a family. I didn't care what it cost. I love children, and I wasn't convinced that God didn't want me to be a mother. I picked up shifts at Perkins to help with the extra bills. I was determined to do anything I could to make my dream of a family come true. Everyone around me seemed to be pregnant, and the feeling of this never happening to me was something I couldn't fathom.

After two long, daunting years of no success, it didn't seem like having children naturally was an option. Next, we researched the option of adoption. My mom was adopted, and I knew other people who adopted children. I was good with it. When we found out that the minimum fee to adopt was $10,000, my husband wasn't all for the idea. We decided to table the idea of starting a family and find something else to focus on, so we elected to buy some land and build a new house. I found myself going from one emotional stress to another. I was missing something in life and could not wrap my mind around not having a family.

We spent a year building what we thought was our dream home. We moved into our new house in November 1997. I loved our new house, but along with the new house came other financial needs, like needing a four-wheeler because it was ten acres. I thought I could put the yearning of having a family to rest, but I couldn't. My older sister just had a baby. My younger sister had two children, and this just didn't seem fair. I felt that all the material things were more of a priority for my husband than adopting a child. I wasn't convinced that we were on the same page. My husband had his ten acres and his toys, and I felt he could give or take the family. I felt he was only going along with it because it was what I wanted. No one I knew really understood what I was going through emotionally and physically just to have a child, except for my good friend from the BGC. I tried so hard, but things were so stressful, and I was so exhausted.

Lisa's new house in Cold Spring

My job was going well. I moved into a new role as a development and volunteer coordinator at the Boys & Girls Clubs. I found myself spending a lot of time at work. My husband also worked long hours. I focused on my job and loved my new house, but I felt empty. We fought a lot, and I needed a break. I was confused and stressed, and I really didn't know my life purpose after trying to come to terms that I wasn't going to be a mom.

I decided to get an apartment in St. Cloud. I continued to work for the Boys & Girls Club. During this time, my Grandpa Olson passed away.

I found out during this time that the Boys & Girls Clubs serving Porter County, Valparaiso, Indiana, was hiring a new position, a development director. In June 1997, I applied for the job, went for an interview, and was offered the job.

* * *

Hans

Life is under no obligation to give us what we expect.
—Margaret Mitchell

There is a sociological phrase called a "significant life event," where something happens that completely changes the direction of your life—such as a marriage, a divorce, a job change, a death, a birth, and the like. That occurred both for my mother and father before I was born, and it changed them so radically that much of who I am now stems from those events.

In 1942, for a twenty-two-year-old German man, military service was basically required. If the propaganda didn't convince you to join, the soldiers patrolling the streets made it clear that if you didn't join, bad things could happen to you and your family. It was a very effective recruitment policy. After three years of having survived the war, mostly on the Russian front, the war ended. During the last part of the war, the Russians used a "scorched earth" method of defense, which consisted of continuous, slow retreat while burning everything behind them. The advancing German army, which was used to utilizing the supplies—such as food and gasoline—from the cities that they attacked, found that there was nothing to use, and they slowly began to starve as they moved forward. In May 1945, my father, Oskar Scheller, was a soldier in the German army, advancing towards Russia, when news came that Adolf Hitler had committed suicide and Winston Churchill had declared victory.

Shortly thereafter, German soldiers and military officers were loaded into boxcars on trains to be transported back to Germany. The main focus was getting everyone back to Germany and not safety. Most of the personnel were excited that a war, which many of them wanted no part of, was finally over and that they were going home.

People were being crowded into boxcars with open doors to fit more people when someone standing by an open door slipped. He was falling from the train. Another soldier reached out to try to grab and keep the person from falling. Unfortunately, this caused the slipping soldier to completely lose his footing and fall from the train. By the time the train could be stopped, both of his legs had been cut off by the wheels of the train, one just above the knee and one just below. The slipping soldier, my father, had come unscathed through the war, yet he suffered a horrific injury on the way home from it.

My mother, Hilde Hoffmann, had her event in the aftermath of World War II. After the war ended, Germany was split into two countries, democratic West Germany and communist East Germany. In 1958, my mother's family decided to cross over the border from East to West Germany. This was not an easy task as there were barbed wire fences and armed patrols guarding the border. It was a dangerous weeklong journey, but they safely made it into West Germany.

The following year, my mother and father met, and I was born on August 24, 1960. Three years later, with difficult economic prospects in Germany, my parents decided to move the family to America.

Nuremberg, Germany

Hans as a little boy

Hans 1962

In October 1963, my parents brought my younger sister, Marion, and me to the airport and boarded a plane with Chicago as our destination. We were going to Chicago because my dad's brother lived about an hour away in Valparaiso, Indiana, and he was our sponsor in the United States. I believe that the difficult events of their lives helped them through this major upheaval. Given what they had already gone through, moving to another country was not a huge undertaking.

While America was thought of as the land of opportunity, it was a long time coming for my family. My dad's brother had a job and a place to live set up for us. That sounds great, but the reality was that my father had no legs, the job was minimum wage, and he had three other mouths to feed. Moreover, we were very slowly learning to speak English by watching PBS television programs like *The Electric Company* and *Sesame Street* on TV every day. It also did not help that President Kennedy was assassinated the month after we arrived in the country, which caused immigrants from any nation to be looked upon suspiciously.

My parents rarely spoke about their lives in Germany and the hardships that they had endured. Life in the United States didn't give my family everything they desired, but it did give them the opportunity to fail or succeed on their own, which was not possible in Germany. Attending a small rural school, I heard the words *Nazi*, *kraut*, and *Jew killer* many times during my years there. Sometimes they were vindictive, but, I believe, most of the time it was based on ignorance.

During my junior year of high school, my history teacher, who knew a little about my history, approached me and asked if I thought that my mom would be willing to speak in front of the class. When I asked her and she said yes, I did not realize how difficult that would be for her. At the time, I did not know a lot about the difficulties that my mom and dad had experienced during the war and afterward. I know now that they did not want to burden their children with the horror stories of their past, so they only talked about it on a surface level. Needless to say, I was stunned when my mom stood in front of the class and talked about my dad's leg amputations, her family's journey through the demilitarized zone, having to eat nothing but potatoes for weeks on end, and having to leave not one but two lives totally behind.

They left East Germany with nothing but the clothes on their backs. They left West Germany to come to the United States with only what would fit in a suitcase. I am pretty sure that the teacher was not expecting this kind of revelation, but it opened some eyes and changed the attitude of the students who were in that class. When my parents and I talked that night, they explained that they really tried to focus on the good things that had happened to us and not the bad things.

Being from a German culture that sees alcohol as a diet staple, I was exposed to alcohol around the age of six. My father and his friends thought that it was funny if they spilled some beer on the kitchen table and had me lap it up like a dog. This progressed to having me drink with them a few short years later, and they would buy alcohol for me in high school to party with my friends, if we stayed at the house and did not leave. They thought that was being responsible, but it also gave us the impression that alcohol was not dangerous.

Hans and his dad

Hans as a child

Hans riding his tricycle

Around the age of three, I was exposed to soccer. My father lost his ability to play soccer, so he became the ultimate soccer dad before that phrase was popular. We used to go into the backyard for hours on end with my dad sitting in a chair. I would be about ten to fifteen yards away, and we would kick the ball back and forth with an unusual twist. I needed to be very accurate with my kicks to him because he sat in a chair and had to stop the ball with his crutches, position the ball, and hit it back to me with those crutches. If I didn't kick it closely to him, I had to chase the ball because I couldn't very well have him do it.

In Northwest Indiana in 1966, there were not a lot of options for leagues like there are now. I soon found myself at age five playing in an under-ten league. Everyone I played with and against was about four years older than me. It was a very, very rough start. But by the time I reached nine years old, it was a completely different story. Playing with older kids for so long helped me when I was competing against my own age group. As a forward, I scored a lot of goals, but after most games, my dad would tell me that I should have scored one or two more goals than I did. It was very hard to please him no matter what I did. My frustration vented itself by my behavior on the soccer field, where I received many yellow and red cards for my anger and rough play.

Hans's house in Valpo as a child

Hans with his family

Hans playing foosball with his dad

I went to camps in high school and had three scholarship offers to play division 1 or 2 soccer. I had grown up with a feeling of inadequacy as a student, athlete, and son. My grades were good, but I never applied myself to get straight As. I was an accomplished soccer player, yet I never did the extra practice to become special. And as a son, I never caused any conflict but was never really totally involved in my family life.

For my grades, I used two words that would allow me to take the easy way for most of my life—*rationalization* and *justification*. Justification was telling myself that the class was hard, so a B was a good grade. Rationalization was saying, "Why do I need to study physics? I will never need it in real life."

While playing soccer, I received a number of accolades for my ability but never my sportsmanship. What happened when the referee couldn't see the play was always legal in my eyes. I provoked opponents physically and mentally to try to get an edge. Anything goes because the *only* thing that mattered was the final score. One time I tripped a player when the referee was not looking, and the player got up and ran over to me to confront me. The referee saw that, and when I fell on the ground like he had punched me, the referee kicked him out of the game. He never even touched me, but I knew that I could get an advantage by acting hurt. The result was that his team had to play shorthanded the rest of the game. For a long time, I regarded this as fulfilling as any goal that I scored. My priorities were pretty messed up even then.

The rest of high school consisted of one steady girlfriend and good grades. I never studied much and actually did not bring home a single book in my senior year. I could have done so much better had I tried, but I just coasted through high school. My first two years, I was short and skinny and did not stand out in any particular way. I was somewhat awkward and introverted, but the summer after my sophomore year, I grew five inches and gained thirty pounds. I started to play volleyball for the high school team and made first team all-conference. Even then, just as with soccer and school, I only used my natural talent and did not push myself to achieve excellence.

Hans's high school graduation

Hans playing soccer

My father had his sights set on Indiana University, which had one of the best soccer programs in the country. They offered to let me be a walk-on in the program because the coach knew me from camps, but I only had marginal success, and there was not going to be a scholarship offer for me.

When I realized that I would not be getting a soccer scholarship and I would have to continue to pay to go to college, I decided that moving back to Valparaiso was the best idea. I decided that I could work while I finished school and that Purdue North Central would be the best for me. I started classes, and my uncle, Roland, helped me get a job.

One day in January, I went to the steel fabrication company where I worked. It was always very cold in the mornings, so I had my cotton gloves on while working at a drill press. Being only twenty at the time and not having any experience, I did not know that it could be dangerous to wear gloves while operating a machine like that. The controls for the press were on the side, and as I went to reach around to turn it off, a string from my glove got caught in the chuck. In a split second, it had grabbed my glove by the thumb and twisted it around the press a few times until it shut off automatically because it was jammed. It was jammed because my severed thumb was keeping it from turning any more. It also would not release to let me remove my hand. After a few other employees were able to free my hand, someone drove me to the hospital while I sat in the passenger seat with a bloody left hand and carried my thumb in the right hand. The doctors thought that it would be a miracle if they could reattach it. Both bones in my arm were broken as the bottom part of my arm and my index finger tendon had also twisted around the press. They tried reattachment, which worked to a certain extent.

Although my thumb and index finger are damaged, they are still attached, and I still have some use of them. I have never felt sorry for myself about this disability because of what had happened to my father. Every time I felt bad about the lack of dexterity in my hand, I only needed to think of him never walking again, and that perspective allowed me to be grateful for what I had. My struggles were not always alcohol-related, and my peace was not always because of recovery.

Hans and his siblings

My parents retired and moved to Arkansas in 1981, and my father built his own dream retirement home there. But in 1983, he passed away. While my mom was visiting us in Indiana, he took his small motor home for a drive and apparently had a heart attack. He lost control of the vehicle, went off the road, and ended up in a pond. The RV sank into the depths of the pond. When we did not hear from my dad, my mom got worried and called the local police to check on him, but they did not find him at the house. The following day, the RV floated to the surface and was seen by a passing motorist. It was never determined if he died due to a heart attack or by drowning.

My dad's life insurance policy set aside $10,000 for the three children and $20,000 for my mom. None of us made wise choices with the new windfall. My brother bought a car and wrecked it after drinking, my sister continued to use drugs, and I decided to finish college but decided not to work while doing it. I was taking the easy way out again.

The relationship between my sister, my brother, and me was not a close one. While my sister and I were only two years apart in age, we had completely different lifestyles. She was very quiet and intellectual, and I was very sports-oriented and arrogant. My brother was seven years younger than I, and had we been closer in age, we might have had more in common.

I had believed my sister was using drugs only occasionally and recreationally, but she was actually more involved than I thought. She tried to stop but couldn't.

She finally quit cold turkey on May 25, 1987. I remember the date vividly because that is the date on her tombstone. Twenty-five years old. Some recreation. When my dad died, it took a lot out of my mom, but when my sister died, it took her heart. Marion was very sweet and innocent but also very naive. She did not have much motivation, as evidenced by the fact that she did not finish high school even though she got outstanding grades. She was also willing to trust and try new things, and she started with marijuana. I did not think that was too awful as I had been exposed to it in college and it did not seem that hurtful. She used her share of my dad's life insurance to have fun and live life casually and not too seriously. Her boyfriend at the time introduced her to cocaine, heroin, and other drugs, and it was apparently one of those or a combination of them that killed her. I wanted to know exactly what it was that she died from, but I was told that they would not waste the money on an autopsy just for a suspected drug overdose, and I could not afford to pay for one.

My sister's funeral was only attended by myself, my brother, my mother, and Marion's husband, whom she had only recently married with a Justice of the Peace ceremony. Just the fact that nobody else came depressed me tremendously, and the fact that her husband was there, whom I considered at fault for her death, made me incredibly angry. I went back to my mom's house, and instead of confronting him and finding out exactly what had happened and what he had to do with it, I drank until I passed out. I could not even stay sober long enough to support my mom after she just buried her only daughter. I continually alternated between being embarrassed, mad at myself, and mad at others. There was no situation in my life that I did not think another drink would make better.

Marion E BRANAM

Oakland Memorial Cemetery
Johnson County, Arkansas

1962-1987

Marion's tombstone

I drove to her funeral from Valparaiso in a state of shock and drove home in a state of inebriation—770 miles' worth. It must have been a good buzz because I was dumbfounded when I received notice about six months later that my driver's license had been suspended. After some research, I realized that I had gotten a speeding ticket in Illinois on the way back from my sister's funeral. I did not remember any of it.

> *I do believe that if you haven't learnt about sadness, you cannot appreciate happiness.*
> —*Nana Mouskouri*

The next dozen years passed relatively uneventfully. I had done what most thirty-somethings did—which was get married, hold a steady job, and drink socially.

From 1986 until 1991, I coached boys' soccer at Valparaiso High School. One of my favorite players was named Jesse, who had decent soccer skills, a fierce determination, and a desire to learn everything he could.

In September 1990, I left that job to become a director at the Boys & Girls Club of Porter County. I went from being the athletic director to the unit director and was very happy in that life.

My drinking at that time was minimal during the week and heavy on the weekends, but I saw some of the effects of alcoholism on a daily level. Some kids had to call their parents at local bars to pick them up when the club closed, and some parents, who lived close enough, walked down to pick up their children. I thought that at least they came to get their kids instead of making them walk home alone, but that thought changed as I saw that many of those parents were almost always drunk when they came to get their kids. Some of the children who attended the Boys & Girls Club were classified as "at risk," which could also mean "living a life in hell." One boy's father showed up almost every night at closing time to pick up his young son and walk home with him. The problem was that his son was always able to walk better than his father, who was always stumbling drunk. Whenever he showed up, I was always disgusted by it and thought of it all the way home after I stopped by the liquor store to get something to drink for the ride home. I didn't even realize the hypocrisy of it.

I met many community leaders, some of whom would also have a major impact in my life in the future. At this point, I had a good job that I loved, good friends, and a comfortable life.

My soccer playing ended when I tore my anterior cruciate ligament in my right knee for the first time in 1995. My knee surgery and having to give up coaching and playing soccer dominated my thoughts instead of the great job, good friends, and world of opportunities I had available. Also, my marriage to my wife was becoming more and more unfulfilling. The fact that I wanted children and she was adamant that she did not want a family was becoming a large issue. If there was a defining time in my life, it was 1997 to 2000.

Significant life events change the direction of your life, but when eleven of them happen over a short period, it is a recipe for disaster. A significant life event can be a marriage, a divorce, a birth, a death, a job loss or change, moving, or anything else that causes a major shift in your life. This was the time frame that I slowly shifted from drinking almost nothing but beer, to drinking only beer socially and vodka privately, and then devolving to rarely drinking beer but drinking vodka heavily and only privately.

Windermere

There comes a time when you need to let go of what you think should be happening and live in what is happening.

Lisa

F ast-forward four years later, and Hans and I were busy caring for our business and two precious daughters . . .

One day, while visiting friends, I stumbled upon some property for sale out in Jackson Township. I called Hans and told him about it. We went to look at it and had his best friend who owned a construction company look at it, and before we knew it, we bought the land to build a new house. I was so excited about the thought of building, and Hans was game for the adventure. We talked about moving to a bigger house wherein we could have our business in the basement. We were looking at the housing market, but there didn't seem to be anything we really liked. I wanted space for the girls to run around. Hans wanted distance between the neighbors. We wanted the girls to be at a good elementary school. What we really liked about the area was that it was a small, family-friendly subdivision. It was close to school, a quiet and wooded lot, and it was centrally located from all the areas we worked our business.

In February 2005, we broke ground on the new house. We were so excited. We took a family vacation to Disney over spring break, we were building a new house, and business was going well. Life was good!

Disney 2006

Florida, 2006

The contractor we'd hired was Hans's best friend for over twenty years, and he was the best man at our wedding. We'd spent a lot of time with him and his wife, going out with them on weekends to Jimmy Buffett concerts, barbecues, etc. When it came to building our house, naturally, we wanted him to do it. Never having built a house before however, we hadn't anticipated how stressful that process would be. There was very little communication between his team and us. Decisions about the property that we hadn't approved of were being made, and it was difficult to connect with him or get any answers, which was very confusing and frustrating. When we were well into the process, we found out he had assigned one of his guys as the lead foreman on our house. Our new foreman got busy doing other things however, and he didn't have time for our house. We were not happy. Hans had trusted his friend to take good care of us, never expecting him to drop the ball.

In October 2005, he demanded that we close on the house even when it wasn't finished, and at the closing, he tried to manipulate the numbers. We had to have an attorney present at the last minute. After the closing, we discovered that the guy he'd put in charge of our house was let go because he was heavily drinking on the job. I know this was a very difficult time for Hans. His best friend had let him down.

The move was more challenging than we'd imagined. This was right before the housing bubble collapsed and mortgage companies were offering generous loans with little proof of income. We had not yet sold our house in Valparaiso, so here we sat with two mortgages, two car payments, and all the utility bills for both homes. What had we gotten ourselves into?

A friend told us about a relative moving here from Florida who might be interested in renting our Valparaiso house. She could not afford the whole mortgage, only three-fourths of it, but we rented it to her anyway. The plan we'd agreed upon was for her to rent-to-own, but within six months, she had destroyed the inside of the house and moved out without notice. We couldn't afford both payments, and the Valparaiso house went into foreclosure.

Despite our financial issues with the move, we were determined to move forward. I tried to be very optimistic. I was busy with the business. Hannah just started first grade, and Delaney was attending Montessori School in Valparaiso. We loved Hannah's new school and her first-grade teacher. I loved the peacefulness of country living. I tried to look for the silver lining and be optimistic about things getting better for us.

When we first moved to Windermere Woods, I was so excited for us to make new friends. Our new neighborhood was small with maybe twenty houses, but more than half of the families had children Hannah and Delaney's age. I quickly became friends with a couple of amazing and fun ladies. One was a stay-at-home mom, and the other was a nurse. I loved hanging out with my new friends. We all came from different backgrounds, but we were very supportive of each other. We were young moms going through the ups and downs of parenting young kids, balancing family life, and wanting to have adult conversations and a little fun. All of us were very involved in the elementary school our children attended. We were room moms and volunteered for all the classroom parties, organized the year-end all-school field day, taught Junior Achievement, and so much more. The school families were our community. Having family get-togethers on weekends became something we all looked forward to. One family would host. We would have dinner, drinks, and games, and the children would play. I loved hosting Halloween, Christmas, birthday parties for the girls, dance parties, sleepovers, and more. I wanted the girls to be happy and enjoy with their friends.

With our adult friends, we planned pub crawls as well as Jimmy Buffet concert trips. We loved getting together with our friends and having a good time. Hans would drink beer, and I would drink wine. We always had a great time with our friends.

Hans was a very involved dad. He loved playing school with the girls, reading to them, coaching soccer, taking them on bike rides, going on trips, and so much more. Friends would comment on what a great dad Hans was and how their children loved spending time with him.

Hans and girls at a Girl Scouts activity

I loved being involved with my friends. A group of neighbor ladies and I signed up for the three-day Breast Cancer Walk. Our subdivision was a great place to train. We would get the kids on the bus and walk a couple of laps around the neighborhood. One day, while walking with my friends, I noticed a number of hard liquor bottles in our neighbor's recycling bin, and I thought to myself, *How could anyone possibly drink that much hard liquor over a two-week period? Or are they cleaning out their liquor cabinet?*

It never dawned on me that that many bottles could indicate a serious addiction problem. It wouldn't be long before my naivete would crumble into a thousand pieces.

Meanwhile, life was stressful inside our four walls. Hans was stressed about paying the bills. Our business was on a downward turn. He tore his Achilles tendon and had surgery, and I was stressed and scared. I started to become more demanding of Hans. I wanted him to fix things and make the situation better. The more scared I got, the more demanding I got, and I started blaming Hans for not taking care of things. We started to get collection notices in the mail, something neither Hans nor I had ever dealt with. Everything felt tense and overwhelming.

Hans spent a lot of time in the basement watching TV and drinking. He said it was his man cave. I couldn't understand why he wouldn't want to be upstairs with the girls and me, enjoying family time. When I went down there to ask him to come up, he became belligerent and sarcastic.

"It is your job to take care of the girls," he would say.

That was a trigger that made me go ballistic. Who would say that? This wasn't the Hans I knew. He loved his girls. I resented Hans for escaping to the basement time and time again because I didn't have the luxury of escaping anywhere.

In September of 2008, I was desperate for something positive for me and the girls and decided to adopt Polly, our goldendoodle, who has been a wonderful addition to our family. Because of our dire financial situation however, I wasn't honest with Hans about how much I paid for her because I knew he'd be angry.

When we first got Polly

That November, my parents made their annual Thanksgiving visit. I always looked forward to our time together. We had created a tradition in which my parents would attend Grandparents' Day at the girls' school on Wednesday, eat Thanksgiving dinner with us on Thursday, and then we'd all go to Chicago together on Friday. It was such a special family event. Little did I know, it would be our last all together.

My mom was not feeling well and was in need of a wheelchair. I'd told my mom she didn't have to come for their annual visit if it was too hard on her, but she said, "Oh no, we are coming. It is tradition!"

As per usual, my parents went to Grandparents' Day, and we cooked Thanksgiving dinner together. Then we rented a wheelchair and went to Chicago. I took her to her favorite yarn shop where she bought bags of yarn to keep her busy when she was to have her new cancer treatment at the Mayo Clinic.

Lisa's mom's last Thanksgiving with us

About a week after my parents were at our place, my dad called and asked us all to come home for Christmas. I didn't ask any questions because I knew when my dad asked something of us, it was important. For the first time in twelve years, all the siblings, spouses, and grandchildren went home for Christmas.

Though my dad didn't talk about it, I had an inkling that my mom's days were numbered. The day after Christmas, she ended up in the hospital, and I remember her saying to me, "Honey, I don't want to die here."

I said, "Mom, you are not going to die. We are just going to get you meds so you feel better."

Sure enough, once they hooked her up to an IV, she was herself again. What a close call. We were happy and relieved as we all headed back to our homes.

Last Christmas with Lisa's mom

On New Year's Eve, we went to some of our friends for their annual New Year's Eve party. The next day, my dad called from the hospital to say my mom had passed away. All of us siblings and our families headed back to my parents. I remember lying in bed, thinking of my mom, and I could feel her presence. She said to me, "Honey, don't worry, I am okay, and you will be okay too."

Since that time, I have had several visits from my mom in my dreams. She always sends a sign to let me know she is still with me and watching over us.

I was back in Minnesota a lot after my mom died—at least once a month. I was worried about my dad. My mom had taken care of all the household things—meals, family gatherings, etc. They had been married for forty-five years, and my mom was his best friend. In March, after returning from his annual Mexico trip, I got a call from dad. He told me about a lady he'd started seeing from the church he and my mom attended. The lady was an acquaintance of my mom's. I was happy for my dad because now he wouldn't be alone. I couldn't be judgmental because it wasn't my life, and I didn't know what my dad was going through. I just wanted him to be happy.

Meanwhile, back in Chesterton, things were slipping quickly. It all looked wonderful on the outside, but on the inside, we were stressed and scared. We felt like we were losing everything. The economy flipped, and we couldn't keep up with the downfall. The mortgage we got on our new house was $150,000 more than what the house was appraised at. We couldn't sell the house, and we couldn't make the payments. We decided to sell Community Connections. We had built the business, and it had some equity. We figured it was enough equity that we could get by for a year and find other jobs in the meantime.

We hired our friend who was an attorney to draw up the papers. We had commitments to the new owners to help with the business transition. I taught the wife how to make the baskets as well as how to do the books, and Hans was supposed to help the husband with the sales side of the business. As time went on, I was getting calls that Hans was not showing up to meet with the guy. Where was he? He would come home, and I would question him on his whereabouts. He would say he was out and that he did meet with the new owner. We would end up in a fight, and Hans would leave. Sometimes he would leave for the night with no contact. I would get so livid.

I knew, for the girls' sake, I needed to maintain normalcy during this difficult time. I would make sure they had playdates with their neighbor friends, went to school, had a routine, and all the holidays and birthdays were celebrated.

If you're going through hell . . . keep going!

All I wanted was a normal marriage and family life. Not really knowing what was "normal," I had this picture in my head of how things should be. I wanted a loving husband who shared the same dreams as mine. I wanted us to have a great business, a nice house, and two healthy children. I wanted to receive back the same kind of love I gave. I believed that if I could make a beautiful home, work hard, take care of the girls, take care of all our finances, cook great meals, and entertain our friends, I would be appreciated and loved more. I expected Hans to respond to all my efforts the way I wanted him to. I tried so hard to make things easy on him. The harder I worked, the less he had to do. But when he wasn't appreciative of all my efforts, I felt disappointed and unloved, and I got angry. I had absolutely no problem letting him know how I felt, and I was not nice about it. I yelled, screamed, stomped my feet, slammed doors, called him names, and did so many other ugly things. I didn't even know myself anymore. The stress of life had changed me.

After we sold Community Connections, we started another business called Partners in Fundraising. We helped nonprofits raise money. We were successful in helping several organizations raise additional funds.

There was a walkathon event we were planning for a local charity. Hans's responsibilities were to organize the vendors. I kept questioning Hans about the event:

"Do we have all the details confirmed?" I asked.

"Yup," he said.

"Are you sure?" I asked again.

"Yes," he said. "Why don't you believe me?"

Something didn't seem right or add up. That night Hans took off and didn't come home.

The next day was the event, and I showed up at the park with a friend where the event was supposed to be, and there were no vendors or anyone there, not even Hans. What the heck? I called Hans, and there was no answer. I kept calling him, and there was still no answer. Hans was nowhere to be found. I hadn't a clue where he was.

One of my friends who was with me at that time was beside herself. She asked, "How does he just not call you? Who does something like this?" I wasn't sure either.

I was in denial that this was even happening. I was so scared. What if something happened to him?

Hans finally came home after being gone for three days. He went to see a friend who was the director of Frontline, a substance abuse treatment center. She had given him a Bible and said maybe he needed to investigate getting help.

I was flabbergasted. I said, "What? You don't need help. We can do this on our own. I can help you. We are stressed because of everything going on in our lives, and this is something we can control."

How could Hans think about himself during what was the most uncertain time of our lives? We couldn't afford treatment. We couldn't afford our house payments, car payments, or any of our other bills. I thought this was just a way for him to avoid dealing with all the stress that I was dealing with as well.

Within a couple of weeks, the couple who bought our business was suing us for breach of contract. What on earth was going on? How could life be getting so out of control?

I started to not want to come out of the house. I felt like a failure. All the walls were starting to close in. I didn't want the girls to know how anxious and scared I was. The more Hans distanced himself, the more I wanted to fix it. There had to be a way out.

> *Learn to trust the journey even when it doesn't make sense. Sometimes what you never expected or dreamed of turns out to be God's plan.*

I called my dad, whom I always called when I had a problem. He was a financial planner, and I was sure he could help me. He said to me, "No one has ever walked in your shoes, and I am going to tell you something you don't want to hear, but you are going to have to consider filing bankruptcy."

Bankruptcy . . . there was no way. If we filed bankruptcy, it was all over. How would we ever rise above this mess? My perfect life was blowing up in front of my face. Could everyone around me see what I was desperately trying to hide? I was afraid because I'd never thought my life would ever go in this direction. I'd never known anyone who had filed for bankruptcy and lost everything. This was not my plan!

Hans and I came to the realization that we had no other option than to seek out a bankruptcy attorney. Where could we look? Definitely not in Porter County—we knew so many people. What if someone found out? How would we rise above it?

Hans decided to call upon a friend who was an attorney he trusted, but he didn't deal with bankruptcies. The friend referred Hans to a guy whose office was in a town twenty miles away. Hans found the nerve to make the call for an appointment. I was scared but knew in my heart this was our only option. We were asked to bring all our debtors. What if we were asking for too much forgiveness?

The attorney's office was nothing fancy. The receptionist had us fill out some paperwork. As we sat there waiting, other people who I assumed were also filing for bankruptcy came in and out. I didn't consider myself in their class of people. Hans and I had great jobs, and we had a successful business. How on earth did we get into this mess?

A lady called us back into a boardroom. We sat down and waited a few minutes for the attorney to come in. The guy came in and shook our hands. We all sat down, and within minutes he made us feel at ease and like he was a friend we had always known. He was very reassuring that we were not the only ones who recently had to make this tough decision because of the recent economic downslide.

Based on our situation, he recommended we file chapter 13. We quickly trusted him and knew everything he recommended was exactly how we were to move forward. I felt awful that we couldn't fulfill our financial responsibilities to our debtors, but our attorney reminded us this was why the bankruptcy options were available. Part of the chapter 13 was letting our beautiful house go. We had no choice. We were not up on our payments, and there was no way we could afford it. Selling it was not an option. We had a $500,000 mortgage on a house the realtors told us we could list for $350,000.

We found we were not the only victims of the 2008 recession. Several other of our friends were struggling, but no one talked about it. We were all doing our best to move forward, hoping for a miracle.

In September 2010, five years after we moved into our beautiful new house, it was time to leave and start a new chapter. It was time to move forward, put our past behind us, and make decisions about our future.

Hans and I were good with everything our attorney told us. We felt a huge load lifted. After we filed bankruptcy, within a couple of months, I had three friends who shared with me their financial difficulties. I was blessed to have had the experience with our attorney so that I could refer them to him. I found out that we were not alone in what we were dealing with.

* * *

Hans

Amazingly, our business prospered to the point that Lisa and I built a half-million-dollar house for the family to grow in. Lenders were basically giving mortgages to anyone, and we qualified for the loan with no money down. Our house in Valparaiso had not sold yet, and the person who was renting it had stopped paying, so it ended up going into foreclosure. We were drowning in debt and didn't even realize quite how much.

The house was supposed to take six months to finish but ended up being nine months. It was two acres of woods in a nice area. We had designed it to be at the back of the property with the trees keeping the house hidden from the road. One day after the foundation was done and they were getting ready to put the septic system in, we went to the house to check it out. Apparently, in order to get the septic system to fit, they needed to do a mound system, and the only place to do it was in front of the house. When we arrived that day, all the trees in front of the house had been taken down. The privacy that we wanted had been replaced by a hill of dirt. We were furious about it among other issues with the house, which resulted in a dissolution of a twenty-five-year friendship with myself and the builder.

Apparently, his job foreman would check out the crew in the morning and spend the rest of the day at a local bar until he had to check it again in the afternoon, and the results showed it. After about two years, a one-and-a-half-inch-wide crack appeared in the living room ceiling, nail pops appeared in the drywall, among other construction issues.

After a year or so, our business started to fail as it was tied to the housing market, which had started to plummet. The thriving business that we had when we bought the house started to dwindle as more and more advertisers pulled out due to the economy.

Lisa was increasingly difficult to live with due to the micromanaging she did. I didn't realize that she was only trying to control me because I couldn't control myself. I knew that I was drinking too much but always rationalized it in some way. I told myself that Lisa was hard to live with, we didn't have enough money, everyone was always on edge, and on and on. I never once looked in the mirror and thought about what I had contributed to these troubles. Life in the house on Windermere Drive was almost surreal. I had never lived in a nicer house, driven nicer vehicles, had more "things," or been as unhappy. The pressure to do well was suffocating me. I used to love to take people on a tour of the house and show it off, not realizing how little that mattered to others, especially the friends who loved us unconditionally. I irrationally felt that showing what we had gave me more worth.

Our adjustable mortgage went to $2,300 per month, and our van was repossessed. Blackouts were starting to happen with regularity. Our income was half of what it used to be and did not look promising.

After the business did sell and we had some money in the bank, instead of regrouping and coming up with a good plan to go forward, we bought a new vehicle and spent ten days at Disneyworld, which took up about half of our money. Our second trip to Florida was even better than the first one. We rented a limousine, which actually did not cost much more than parking at the airport. With the girls being older, they could enjoy all the parks and rides.

Hannah adores her daddy

Limo to airport for Disney trip

There were many nights that I picked a fight with Lisa just so I could leave the house and park somewhere, usually the parking lot by the toll road. I always had a bottle handy to take with me, and I did this even on nights when the temperature got to zero degrees. Those were nights I did not know if I would wake up in the morning and didn't really care. Lisa and I would have huge arguments in front of the girls, who were going through their own personal hell throughout these years. They rarely got mad at me when they were younger because I think they were confused as to why their parents would act this way, or maybe they just thought it was how every family was.

Occasionally, there was a convergence of people, places, and things all at the same time, and they always turned out badly.

My favorite entertainer at the time was Jimmy Buffett, and his concerts were huge parties, which was a great time for most people. The last Buffett show I saw started with a party at our house in Windermere with a tiki bar and lots of margaritas. Most people dress up for a Buffett concert in grass skirts, coconut-shell bras, and tropical attire. I wanted to do something different. I thought it would be a great idea to wear a Corona-bottle-cap bra, but I could not figure out a way to make one that would work. With the brilliance afforded me by a few margaritas, I decided that I needed to put on the bottle caps without all the string to make a bra, so I used a hot glue gun, filled the bottle caps, and attached them. Even drunk, you can experience excruciating pain, but it was nothing like the pain of removing them the next day while sober. Probably the most puzzling thing is that after the pain of putting on the first one, I had no problem with doing it again.

One great thing did happen at that time, and it was when Lisa brought home a goldendoodle puppy we named Polly. The price that she told me she paid was about half of what it really was because she knew that I would never spend a lot of money on a dog. Polly is still with us, and she was there every day during my good times and most importantly my bad ones. In many instances, she helped me get through the tough times. That is not to say she was awesome all the time.

One afternoon when Lisa was gone she left a loaf of banana bread on the counter. Lisa came home and got mad at me when she discovered that the loaf was gone. I had been drinking a lot, and I really couldn't remember if I had eaten it or not. The mystery continued until later that evening when the bread reappeared on the living room floor, half digested, and I swear that Polly had a huge grin on her face.

That fall, Lisa's mom, Shirley, became more ill with a final diagnosis of colorectal cancer. Her dad specifically asked us to go there for Christmas, and we knew that it could be her last one. While Lisa's relationship with her had been rocky at times, the last few years had been a very close one for them. I think Lisa's mom realized that it was family and not material things that really mattered, and she became a very strong influence in our girls' lives. Even though it was only a few years, she made a huge impact on the girls, and they remember her vividly and the things they did together. She was a very strong woman with a difficult upbringing due to her own adoption, but in the last years of her life and the first few years of Hannah's and Delaney's, she passed on her strength. To this day, both of the girls show those characteristics.

One afternoon I was coaching soccer at an indoor arena for an under-fourteen travel soccer team when I pushed off with my foot and I felt a sharp pain in my left foot. I tried to stand up but couldn't, and when the team trainer checked on me, he said that I had ruptured my Achilles tendon, which I believed due to the large lump by my left calf. I needed to have surgery and had a dilemma. I was not supposed to eat anything and was supposed to drink only clear liquids before the surgery. I also knew that I should not drink alcohol before the surgery, so I only drank a pint of vodka instead of a fifth, and it was a clear liquid, so I considered that a fair compromise on my part. I even wondered why I was extremely groggy when I awoke from surgery. During my recovery, I had to hide my vodka better since I was not very mobile. Occasionally, Lisa would find a bottle, and I would always say that it was one from a long time ago that I'd forgotten to throw away.

Lisa and I were trying to make money by doing fundraisers for local nonprofits. We had one scheduled for April, only I did not do anything to help run it. I knew that when Lisa and the group we were fundraising for showed up no one else would—no participants or donors. I was mad at myself but mostly just could not face her. I left and holed up in a room that we used as an office in downtown Chesterton for a couple of days until I decided to go home. I went home with my tail between my legs and more vague promises.

That fall, we were foreclosed on and had to find another place to live. I kept on finding ways to avoid living instead of embracing it. I knew that I had demons, but it was easier to try to drown them and avoid them instead of confronting them. I was never good at confrontation in any manner, and if I addressed my drinking, I knew that it would be painful physically and mentally.

With all our mismanagement of money, we decided to file for chapter 13 bankruptcy and contacted someone who was referred to us. He became almost a counselor to us, with no judgment but only patience and understanding. During the Windermere years, I took advantage of everything that I could. I felt that if someone else did something for me, that was great because I didn't have to do it myself. It ended up with me taking and not giving in every aspect of my life.

Washington Township

Lisa

L eaving Windermere Woods was bittersweet, but the timing was perfect. We found a beautiful new house to rent to own in Washington Township, which was smaller but the right size for us. We felt very blessed for our new beginning.

The girls started attending Discovery Charter School. Hans had just started a new job selling cars, and I got a new job outside the house working for a child-care center where the girls could come to work with me.

On the plus side, we loved our new house, the girls were going to a great school, I had awesome friends, and we started attending church more regularly. There were some challenges, however. Hans liked his job, for example, but like any sales job, the pay was commission-based and was inconsistent. I liked my new job as well, but the pay wasn't great.

During and after the move, we had to sell a lot of our personal items to cover the bills. I was doing my best to keep up with all the finances and make sure the girls didn't go without, but it was a true struggle. I started getting resentful toward Hans for not working harder and bringing home more money. Could we really afford this new life? Had we taken on too much again? We were careful to hide our struggles and act like everything was fine.

Dear God, please help us through this mess. Why do all these challenges keep happening to us?

Faith isn't about asking God to stop the storm. Faith is about trusting God to help you through the storm. Just believe!

One morning, I had just dropped the girls off at school. When I got home, I received a call from Hans's boss that Hans was complaining of chest pains, so they called an ambulance and rushed him to the hospital.

Was it a heart attack?

His dad had died of a heart attack, so my mind was racing as I drove to the hospital. After several tests on his heart and other tests, all the results came back negative.

Thank God for that. But what was causing the chest pain? Stress? Anxiety? How are we going to afford this hospital visit? Hans doesn't have insurance.

After five months of trying to stay afloat with our new home, we needed to reevaluate again. We got behind on rent from Hans being in the hospital and out of work, and it was a struggle to keep up with the basic bills. Not only could we not afford the rent, but we let our chapter 13 lapse. What the heck? Again, on the outside, everything looked great, but on the inside, we were unraveling.

Picture of Washington Township house

Making gingerbread houses

Hannah's first Communion

Delaney's Bible recognition

Lisa sending notes to the girls to remind them how much they are loved

* * *

Hans

We were still living on the edge, but we rented the most expensive place we could afford, which turned out to be for four months before we were asked to leave. I was still in the mindset that we deserved better.

I had now found a position selling cars. What little self-respect I had was lost after just a few weeks on the job. Intense pressure, backstabbing, and deceit were daily events. During a snowstorm that dropped almost twenty inches of snow, we were expected to come in to work and stay until closing even though no customers came in. Not surprisingly, no one wanted to take a test-drive in a blizzard. A thirty-minute drive home that night took almost two hours.

We did have some good times while we lived in Washington Township.

One snowy day, I tied the girl's sled to the back of our car and slowly pulled them through the subdivision. There was no traffic, and they had a great time.

One evening, a customer called from about ninety minutes away to ask if we still had a certain vehicle on the lot. It was a somewhat rare BMW M3. I said yes, and the customer scheduled an appointment for the next day to look at it. The next morning, the vehicle sold, and I told the manager that I was going to call the customer to say not to come, but he said not to, that maybe I could flip them to another vehicle, maybe an Impala. Either way, it was no loss to the company. The customers came in and were extremely upset that I had not called to save them the drive. Needless to say, they did not buy an Impala.

That night when I drove home, I was having a hard time comprehending every aspect of my life. It was now a complete lie—from work to how I treated my family and friends. Everything I said and did was to further advance my life without any regard to the truth.

Washington Township House

Farmhouse

You are braver than you believe, stronger than you seem, and smarter than you think.

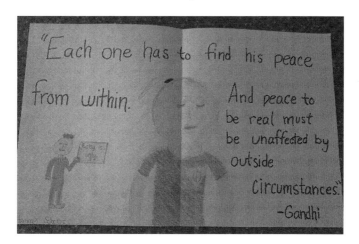

A picture Hannah made Lisa

H ans heard from a friend that there was a small farmhouse available to rent in Chesterton. The rent was half of what we were paying for our Washington Township home. The farmhouse was "old-feeling." The flooring was uneven, the carpet was outdated, there was paneling on the walls, the rooms were small, the windows were drafty, and it had a stale smell. It felt below our usual standard of living, but it was a roof over our heads, and it was only going to be temporary.

Hans was working a lot of hours and didn't have the time to move us himself, so we had a moving company give us an estimate. The estimate of the move was $1,500, and we believed we could afford this. When the day came for the move, the girls were in school, and Hans was at work. It was just me at the house with the movers, who had started loading the truck at 8:00 am. I worked just as hard as the guys loading the truck to get things moved by the end of the day. At 3:00 pm, I left to pick up the girls from school, and when we came home, we were surprised to discover they hadn't made much of a dent in the loading.

The mover in charge seemed perplexed. "We need to move all this tonight?" he asked.

I said, "Yes, it was all a part of the estimate."

He then called in another truck. It was 5:00 p.m. and dark outside when we finally headed to the farmhouse. It had been snowing all day on and off, and the roads were slick. Afraid of getting stuck, the movers refused to go down the long and narrow driveway.

There I was—sitting in the car on a dark country road across our new home with Hannah, who was scared, mad and vomiting and Delaney, who was running a fever. The girls were only eight and ten at the time, and I could not leave them unattended. We desperately needed Hans's help, but he was at work and couldn't be there until 10:00 p.m. Everything we owned was in the two moving trucks—including our beds, clothes, toiletry stuff, etc.

One of the guys came over to my car and said, "We are going to have to park the moving trucks and unload on Monday."

Oh my gosh! I was beside myself! *Monday*—NO WAY! *This can't be happening. This was not a part of the plan.*

When Hans finally arrived, he told the movers we absolutely needed the trucks unloaded that night. We couldn't be in the house directing the movers as to where to put things because we couldn't get to the other end of the driveway. In three hours, the trucks were unloaded, and everything was thrown in the house. Furniture was broken, boxes were split open, and there was no rhyme or reason to the unloading. It was midnight when the movers finally left, and we were standing in the house with boxes piled to the ceilings and mattresses in the kitchen, unable to find sheets or blankets for the night.

What on earth did we get ourselves into? I lay there asking myself after carving out a space for our mattresses in the living room, right before seeing a mouse run across the floor . . . *Oh my god! Welcome home!*

The next day, we finished moving the miscellaneous things from the Washington Township house to the farmhouse, and I set it all up the best I could so it felt like a home. As a kid, I'd loved being on my grandparents' farm and pretending I was Laura Ingalls Wilder from Little House on the Prairie. I actually enjoyed country living, and the girls were adapting well to the new living arrangements. As long as we were all together as a family, they were happy. I was busy working, and the girls were busy with school. In my mind, this was just a temporary transition and we could push through.

Hans got a bill from the movers for $4,000. We were beside ourselves. How on earth could that seven miles move from Washington Township to the farmhouse be an additional $2,500 from what they quoted us? We went ahead and paid the $1,500 but refused to pay the additional $2,500, which we didn't have anyway.

One day in April, after living in the farmhouse for a couple of months, I came home from work and got a call from Hans's boss asking if I knew where Hans was.

I said, "I thought he was at work."

But he said they hadn't seen him.

My god, I thought. *Where could he be? What is he up to?*

I tried calling his cell phone, but there was no answer. At around 4:00 p.m., Hans finally called me back.

"Where are you?" I demanded, both angry and concerned.

"I am at the Michiana Behavioral Health Center in Plymouth," he told me. "I have checked myself in for detox. I went to see someone at Frontline, and she said this is where I need to be," he said.

I was floored. All I could think about was how selfish it seemed for him to just up and leave his family with no discussion and without asking for my input. How were we going to move forward? This was an absolutely terrible time for Hans to be thinking of himself. How was I going to afford everything on my own? If Hans didn't work, he wouldn't get paid. He didn't have insurance to cover this kind of treatment. I felt abandoned. What was I going to tell the girls?

Oh my gosh, this can't be happening! Who just walks out on their family? This isn't the Hans I know. Who am I going to call and talk this through with?

I felt so alone. I finally reached out to my older sister. After talking it over with her, I came to the realization that Hans wasn't being selfish by what he had done. It took a lot of nerve and determination to admit he had a problem then drive himself over an hour to check himself into a hospital by himself. Hans was grasping for help. He wanted to get physically and emotionally better for his family. How long was he going to be gone? Hans said it would be a weeklong program, but it could be less if he showed improvement. A week? What? How was I going to make it?

Please show improvement and come home, I thought. *I didn't sign up for this life, and neither did the girls.*

There I was back in Chesterton, all alone, trying to take care of everything by myself. When I picked the girls up from their friends' house, I tried my best not to act overly concerned. I just told the girls that their dad was away getting help. Fortunately, I had a village of friends who helped me with the girls and with many other things I didn't know how to take care of. I kept telling myself this was temporary. I could do this. I had no choice. I had to rely on others, which wasn't easy for me. I was living the single-parent life and trying to adapt to a new norm. God placed people in our lives who stood in the gap of the darkness without questions or judgment.

Girls and Lisa when Hans was gone

Easter when Hans was in rehab in Plymouth

One of my friends was aware of Hans's struggle with alcohol, and she was the one I called when I found out Hans left and checked into a rehab hospital. She helped me with the girls. She knew well the pain that addiction could wreak on a family. She was a rock to me during the years our family went through the nightmare of this disease. She was there for Hannah and Delaney. She took them overnight. She was compassionate, always there with a listening ear. My friend and her husband even made a few hard phone calls when I couldn't. She never turned her back on me, nor did she prevent our girls from being friends because of our family issues. As for the girls' friendship, it didn't matter if we lived in a beautiful big house where they first met or here at the farmhouse. The girls' friendship was deeper than that. God put this family and friendship in our lives because he knew that was what we needed, and we are truly blessed.

While driving the girls to school, I would pray, "Please, God, show me a sign that you are with me."

And God never let me down. Throughout the day, something would happen that showed his presence. I would get the mail, and a bill would be forgiven. A check would come from the mortgage company in regard to our house on Windermere. Easter came while Hans was gone, and a friend invited us over for dinner and an egg hunt. When I looked for the positive, the silver lining, I could always find it.

The hospital released Hans within ten days and said he showed much improvement and was doing well. The girls and I were excited to have Hans home. He looked great; he was happy and ready to take on the world. Hans went back to work selling cars, but the day he came back, he was let go with no explanation. It was another unexpected disappointment. What more could we take? How were we ever going to get ahead?

Chaos struck our family once again. I was working, and the girls were going to school. Hans was working for a friend doing landscaping, and he started refinishing again. When we'd all come home at the end of the day, Hans would be critical and mean. What on earth was with him? Every night he would sit outside by himself drinking Gatorade.

"I need space," he'd say. "I am tired."

I was tired too after working all day but still had to take care of dinner, helping with homework, and putting the girls to bed. Some nights Hans would go on a rampage. It was unnerving and unsettling. Where was this erratic behavior coming from? The girls were so scared, and so was I. I didn't know this Hans. I would hold the girls and tell them I loved them and would never leave them. Many nights, Hans would sleep in the girls' room and the girls would sleep with me.

We had very little extra money, and the farmhouse was not a place you wanted to hang out at for very long. The landlord was constantly over at the house, cutting the lawn and in our business.

During the summer months, we spent a lot of time traveling to New Buffalo and St. Joseph, Michigan. Our family loved the outdoors, the beach, and all the awesome things to do in these small towns. We felt we were on vacation for the day, and we could do it with very little money. The day would start out great, but as the day went on, Hans would get agitated, moody, sarcastic, and mean. What the heck? I would tell him we were all in this together. His mood swings were unbearable, and I would react negatively to his behavior. All I wanted was for our family to have fun together and make good memories.

The girls and Lisa in New Buffalo

St. Joseph, Michigan, family trip

After Hans came back from rehab, they sent him home with meds but no follow-up plan. He was struggling. I took Hans to a local doctor, thinking we could get some help or be pointed in the right direction.

The doctor said to us, "It is easy. Just stop drinking, and everything will be fine. I don't drink, and you shouldn't either."

What kind of logic and advice was that to an alcoholic? Easier said than done. We left the clinic with no direction.

We got through the summer of 2011, but by August, we found ourselves not being able to afford the rent payment. All the medical bills, the movers' bill, and the loss of Hans's job was catching up with us. Once again, we went back to see our bankruptcy attorney. Once again, he was very helpful and nonjudgmental. He told us we could put into our bankruptcy the past medical bills, the mover invoice, and all the other items we were unable to pay.

During this time, I had to dig deep to conjure up any strength or faith. We knew the farmhouse was full of negativity, and no one in the family was happy there. But where were we going to go this time?

I remember seeing on Facebook that my friend's sister had been living in their basement but had just moved out. Would they possibly let us rent their basement for a month or two while we reevaluated our life's direction? The husband had been a longtime friend of Hans's. They played soccer together for many years.

I called the wife, and she said, "I was just praying on how we could use that space. Of course, you can stay here. It is only one-bedroom but spacious."

Oh my gosh, another prayer answered. Thank you, Lord!

We decided to put all our things in storage for a couple of months and only take with us our personal items and clothes. Once again, we called movers—not the same movers, of course. I took the day off from work and brought the girls to school while Hans was supposed to be at the house directing the movers as they started loading the trucks. When I returned, the movers were there, but where was Hans? I found him bent over and vomiting; he couldn't get up.

Oh my god, I can't believe this is happening. Not today, not the day of the move. How am I going to do this again by myself?

"Please, Hans, you need to help me," I begged.

He was drinking "Gatorade" again and was so out of it.

I had to find the strength to direct the movers on packing and loading the truck when we went to the storage units. I made Hans go with. I was so angry with him, and as the day went on, he became more incoherent. Was he drinking? How could he have been? Surely, he wouldn't do this to me and the girls! If he was, where did he get it from? Oh my god, this couldn't be happening! It was me, the movers, and Hans drunker than I had ever seen him.

Around 7:00 p.m., the girls were spending the night with their friends, and there was still one more load to unload at the storage units. Hans was passed out, so I called my good friend, who willingly came to help me. She was a lifesaver. We ended up getting everything unloaded by 10:00 p.m. in the pitch-dark space. After we unloaded the last of the items, we went to have something to eat at Jimmy Johns. My friend could see the look of despair, resentment, and sadness on my face.

"What are you going to do?" she asked. I hardly ate anything, and she said, "Lisa, you've got to eat to keep your strength up."

I was beyond exhausted. I was so thankful to my friends for standing in the gap once again.

Farmhouse

Don't look back. You're not going that way!

* * *

Hans

Our next stop was an old farmhouse that we could afford but was dilapidated and depressing. We had movers come since I was at work, and it was a bad snowstorm. They had quoted us $1,500 to move us about seven miles, but since there was a storm and it was a long one-lane driveway, it took them longer. I got home, and he gave me a bill for $4,000, which I told him I could not pay. He told me to pay him or he would have his men load up the trucks and either wait there until I did pay or leave with all our belongings. I wrote a check for the original $1,500, and we had to pay off the rest.

The farmhouse was dirty and not well maintained. There were mice, and there was one bathroom that we could not use as the toilet and shower did not work. Lisa and the girls tried to do the best that they could.

One weekend, Lisa took the girls and some of their friends to a hotel in a neighboring town to celebrate Hannah's birthday. I would celebrate with them and go home so they could have girls' time.

That June we had a beach day planned, but Lisa and I were arguing, probably about something trifling. I got mad and slammed a kitchen cabinet door but realized very quickly that I had not removed my hand from the frame fast enough. The result was that the end of my finger was smashed and barely hanging on by the skin. I went to the bathroom and rinsed off the blood to see how bad it was. I was not sure that it could be reattached. I knew that we had to go to the hospital, but before we could do that, I grabbed a bottle from my bathroom hiding spot and chugged about half of it, using it as my own personal anesthetic, and announced to Lisa that she had to drive me to the hospital. It was sewn on with about ten stitches, but it had some nerve damage, which still bothers me today.

There is nowhere you can be that isn't where you're meant to be.

—*John Lennon*

I didn't go to work one morning but parked at the library. As I sat in the car, I realized that I was only a few blocks away from an organization that specialized in addiction recovery for people ages eighteen to thirty-five. The executive director was also married to a good friend of mine from my soccer days with whom I had fallen out of contact. She met with me immediately, and as we talked, I knew that I had a long road ahead of me and that it would not be easy. The organization was faith-based, so she gave me a copy of *The Life Recovery Bible*, which incorporates the twelve steps of AA.

After I arrived in Plymouth, I called Lisa and told her where I was at. Lisa responded with anger and frustration with me. I was so wrapped up in my own issues that I didn't understand she had issues of her own, which my addiction was making even worse for her, in addition to basically raising our daughters by herself.

Recovery Bible

Everything about recovery was new to me, and I really had no concept of the effort I needed to put into becoming healthy. My time spent at the rehab center included two days of detox, many group meetings that I barely understood, evenings spent watching *Scared Straight!* I was also trying to figure out that if rehab was supposed to be successful, why were some of the other patients going through their fifth or sixth rehab?

Lisa called the manager at the car dealership, who said that I would be welcomed back when I completed my time. When I was released, I was clearheaded and wanted to stop drinking. However, I did not realize what kind of effort was needed in order to accomplish that and what roadblocks were in my way. That was evident to me as soon as I got in the car at the rehab center to drive home and found a ten-dollar bill in the center console. Within a mile, I had stopped at a liquor store and wondered to myself if anyone else had ever relapsed in less than five minutes after leaving rehab.

Upon my return home to the farmhouse, Lisa was cool toward me and did not understand why I had left. She looked at it as me abandoning the family. The next day, I got dressed and left for work. When I arrived, the manager called me into his office. I thought that I might get support and encouragement, but he brought out a sheet of paper for me to read and said that I was being terminated immediately. I asked him about the conversation he had with Lisa, and he said that he was not allowed to tell me over the phone that I was going to be fired. Then he told me to pack up my desk and leave. I did the walk of shame in front of the other employees, packed up, and drove home. At least I intended to drive home, but I stopped at the liquor store and picked up a fifth of vodka. I had to stop on the way home because the bottle I had hidden in the bathroom at work had been discovered and was gone.

On my way home, I had decided that my life was worthless, and so was I. I was going into depths that I had not even thought possible. I was going back to the farmhouse. The girls were at school, and Lisa was at work. I would be alone for the whole day. I was thinking dark thoughts and did not know exactly where they would lead. Amazingly, when I got home, Lisa was there and kept me from more negative thinking.

A friend and his wife that I knew from my soccer playing days were there to help us as we needed to move again. They had a finished basement that we could stay in. The day that we were supposed to move our belongings into storage and move our clothes to our friends' basement, I was drunk again as I could not confront another failure on my part. A few years before, we were building our houses at the same time and had a bet on who would move in first. We won that bet, but now our house was gone, and we had to live in their basement.

As Lisa and a different moving company took our belongings into storage, I was passed out on the floor of a room in the farmhouse that we never used, and the girls were at school. I would neither have been surprised nor blamed her if Lisa had left me there.

Our Friends' Basement

Lisa

Faith is thanking God in the storm, trusting he has your back in the valley, and taking his lead in the darkness.

In August 2011, we moved to our friends' basement. It had one bedroom (in which we crammed a queen-size bed and a set of bunk beds), a half bathroom with a sink and toilet, a small kitchenette with a dorm refrigerator and small sink, a living room, and a separate entrance from outside. This was the beginning of our new normal. I would go to work, and the girls went to school. Hans got himself a part-time job at Kellogg's, and he was working on his sobriety. Our friends made us feel like family. We had a roof over our head, food on the table, clothes to wear, a car to drive, and the girls were happy. Our basic needs were met.

I talked to Hannah and Delaney about their dad's illness. When Hans had been drinking, I would say, "Your dad's disease is acting up." They knew when he had been drinking because Hans and I would fight a lot and he would be critical of the girls. We'd come home and find him passed out in bed or on the couch. He'd smell stale like he hadn't showered in days.

It was time to get back to church. Our pastor had retired from the Lutheran church, and we tried to go back after he left, but the community didn't feel the same. The friends we were living with invited us to attend their Presbyterian church. We attended the third service, which was a contemporary service. The praise band was awesome. The people were so friendly. We knew some other familiar faces from the community, and we connected with the pastors. We quickly became very involved. We felt like we belonged. The church's mission was, "We don't care where you have been. We care where you are going." We needed this in our life after filing for bankruptcy, struggling with Hans's alcohol addiction, and enduring so many upheavals. We started to meet people who had been where we had been, people who also wrestled with addiction. It was comforting to not feel alone. Going to church and getting involved was a blessing. We were exactly where we needed to be. We loved that Hannah got involved in a youth group with some amazing leaders and mentors and that Delaney was making new friends in Sunday school.

Delaney serving at church

Christmas, December 2011

Hans really connected with the pastor and his sermons. They developed a great relationship. The pastor invited Hans to be a part of a recovery group that met at the church once a week. He was like the father figure Hans never had, taking him under his wing and becoming his confidant. Hans wasn't brought up in the church. He was baptized Catholic, but after that, church wasn't a priority in his life. He went to church because I thought it was important. Growing up, I got my Sunday hour fill at the Lutheran Church but didn't have time or make time for church outside of the Sunday morning service, until we had the girls. Becoming a mother prompted a desire for my girls to grow up in the church, to know Jesus and the Bible.

At the Presbyterian Church, we were introduced to a couple who had been through addiction. They are such a loving Christian family. The couple was more than ten years younger than us, but their story was similar to ours. The husband was in the praise band, and he was a lay pastor. This amazing couple has been a blessing to our family. I quickly became good friends with the wife. When I shared with my friend what was going on or what I had dealt with, she knew exactly what to say because she had already walked this journey. My friend and I worked the nursery at church on Sunday mornings, and I so much looked forward to our conversations. It was better than going to counseling. I would take in everything she shared with me because she had already come out of the dark valley; she was my hope. She was the first one I called when things were going awry at home. She would check on myself and the girls.

The husband was a good friend to Hans. He took him to AA meetings and went out to coffee with him. He was someone Hans could really talk to. He helped Hans try and understand the disease. I was so thankful for him because he helped take some of the pressure off me. I felt God was really watching over us when he put this couple in our life. Finally, people who understood us and we could relate to. This disease was not just our family secret anymore.

I was blessed with another good friend during this time. Her daughters became friends with my girls. While at one of the girls' track meets, we started talking about Hans's drinking. My friend shared with me that she and her husband were both recovering alcoholics, as was her dad. She and her family became a huge source of support for our family. She would take the girls overnight, and her husband reached out to Hans and tried to talk to him. Her dad went to AA meetings with Hans. This friend was someone that I could spend endless hours talking to. I would pick her brain about what to do. Her family went above and beyond for us. Hannah and Delaney knew that this family was a safe haven, and if they needed anything, they could go to them.

I've never felt comfortable sharing my problems with others, going to a counselor, or speaking in groups. Church became a place I felt safe and welcomed. The people were not judgmental. While we lived in our friend's basement, things were finally starting to feel a little normal: work, school, school activities, and Sunday church. Our friends made us feel like family. Hans's friend was another good sounding board for him (and was a distraction for me.) I was now able to focus on me and the girls. I could clear my head and breathe. I didn't feel like I was on demand all the time.

We bought a new car, an Equinox, and things were going well until one morning in December when Hans dropped me off at work, the girls off at school, and headed back to the house. I got a call from Hans, and I could hardly hear him.

"I got in an accident," he said.

What on earth? It had not been snowing, and the roads were clear.

"Where are you?" I asked.

"On a country road."

I could not leave work and get to him because he had dropped me off, so I called the police, and Hans got a hold of his friend. I was so thankful to him for picking Hans up. I wasn't sure what happened. Were the roads icy? Could have Hans been drinking that early in the morning? When I asked him what happened, he blew me off as if it was no big deal.

The plan was to live with our friends for a short period of time as Hans worked on his sobriety, he looked for a stable job, and we could find our own place to live. I wanted my family back intact and not living as though we were not competent. Hans was working fifteen to twenty hours a week. I was working forty-eight hours a week at a child-care center. Neither of us was making much to support our family. How were we going to get out from underneath this mess? Right in front of my eyes, my life was slipping downward again, and I had no control.

The last year really was starting to weigh on me. I had fought to stay strong for Hans and the girls for so long, but now I was exhausted and starting to despair and lose hope. I was in my darkest days . . . I would often ask, "How could life get any worse?" God gave me two beautiful girls, and it was my job as their mother to take care of them. I was trying to juggle so much. "Please, God," I begged, "give me the strength."

Hans continued to drink. He tried to hide it, but I started to recognize the signs of his drinking. The day would start out great, but then by midmorning, our conversations would start to go awry, or he wouldn't answer his phone. Many afternoons, I would come home from work, and he would be passed out with our dog Polly lying right next to him. Other times, he'd just disappear, and I wouldn't know where he was. I tried to control his drinking by giving him very little access to money. When he did have money, he needed to be accountable and show me his receipts. I knew where every penny was, or so I thought. I also thought if I kept him busy by having him drop off and pick up the girls from school, running errands, and all the other chores, he would stay sober. Never did I think he would drink and drive when the girls were in the car. I worked from home, and I found myself checking on him a lot. The trust between us was very minimal. I would call him when I thought he was running late. I asked him to call me when he left somewhere and when he arrived somewhere. If I thought that he was taking too long, I would call him. I wish I'd had access then to the Find My Friends app.

One day I came home from work, and Hans was in bed. I knew he had been drinking all day.

"Hans, what are you doing?" I asked in frustration. "Why do you continue to do this to us?"

"I just want to get better," he would say. "I don't want to do this anymore," he would mumble.

I was beside myself. I called my sister Sheila, crying. "Hans needs help but doesn't have health insurance, and I don't know what to do."

She said, "There must be some inpatient place he can go."

I googled rehabs and found Regional Mental Health Center. I had never done this before. I didn't know what questions to ask.

The intake lady on the other end asked me several questions, and I answered them the best I could.

She said, "I am not sure what we have available, I'll get back to you."

I prayed, "Please, God, help us!"

I received a callback, and she said, "We have an opening at our Regional Mental Health Center in East Chicago."

East Chicago, I thought. *How am I going to get him there? Is it going to be a decent place? I can't tell the girls. What am I going to tell the girls? How am I going to tell our friends that we need to stay longer? How can this be happening?*

We lived in a basement, pretty much homeless. What was supposed to be a six-week stay at our friends until we regrouped had turned into seven months with no end in sight. There were so many unanswered questions.

"God, please give me the strength to help Hans," I prayed.

I told Hans they had an opening at the hospital and I could take him there the next day.

> *God has not called you to fit in but to stand out in your gifting and your purpose. (1 Peter 2:9)*

After being up all night, making sure Hans didn't take off and disappear again, we got ready to leave for the rehab hospital. East Chicago was a forty-minute drive. I definitely had to drive because Hans was in no position to. East Chicago wasn't an area I was familiar with other than that was where the casinos were from when I had my basket business.

Hans and I got to the inpatient center, which looked like a hospital. We walked in and told the front desk we were there. The environment was very cold. Hans was very quiet, somber, and pretty much lifeless. I was feeling very helpless and alone but also knew we were exactly where we were supposed to be. Hans and I got called back to registration, and I was bracing myself for how much the cost was going to be without insurance. We went through the paperwork. They asked Hans to give me all his personal belongings and said it was time to say goodbye. Hans went one way, and I went the other way. It was time for me to get in the car and head back to Chesterton alone. I got in the car and started driving while tears rolled down my face. There I was, going back to that basement apartment to carry on with a new normal that was so uncertain. What was I going to tell the girls? I called my sister and told her I was so scared to be a single parent. I hadn't signed up for that.

She said, "Lisa, you can do this. Hans is exactly where he needs to be, and you have been a single parent for the last year." Her words gave me strength. "I can do this! God is with me."

What I knew for sure was that the rehab program was thirty days. My plan was to keep things as normal as I could for the girls. I got home and shared with the girls that their dad was in the hospital getting help with his illness. I told them it was my job to go to work, their job to go to school and do their personal best, and that Dad's job was to get better. I needed to keep my strength up. I felt a sense of relief that I didn't have to worry about what Hans was doing all day. But my next worry, of course, was how were we going to afford it. My sister once again told me there were resources available for us and our income level.

"I can't ask for help," I said.

She assured me that was what they were there for, to help people who couldn't afford the treatment.

"You have paid taxes," she said.

My sister convinced me it was what I needed to do. I never imagined I would be signing up for SNAP (food assistance) and Healthy Indiana Medicaid for the girls. What was life coming to?

Lisa and the girls 2012

The girls had spring break at the end of March, and it was a perfect time for us to take a trip to Minnesota to see my dad, sister, and brother. I needed to have a break from all that was going on in Indiana, and I wanted the girls to be with family. It was exactly what we needed to break up the craziness we were living.

After our trip to Minnesota, Hans had maybe two weeks left in rehab. He seemed to be doing well and was on a very routine schedule. He was able to call us once a day. The girls sent him letters, and he in return sent letters to us.

Hans shared with me that as a part of the program, they offered a family day. We would get to see Hans and how he was doing. Maybe they would have us do a family craft, and we'd have cookies and juice. The girls would get to give their daddy a hug. It was hard for the girls not to see their dad.

Family day arrived, and the girls and I drove to the Regional Mental Health Center. The girls were excited but a little apprehensive, and I found myself reassuring them that everything was going to be okay, even though I was feeling apprehensive myself. I tried to be upbeat and positive, but really, it was overall depressing, and my mind was in a thousand places.

We were brought into this gymnasium. It was dark and dingy, with chairs arranged in a big circle. There was a gentleman who talked to all the family and friends ahead of time. Besides the girls and me, there were about five to ten people there visiting. My girls were the only children. What was I doing, bringing the girls to such a daunting place? In my mind, this family day had not looked like this.

I was surprised to see Hans. He had shaved his head and looked very different. Many people who were in the group for treatment were court-ordered, and Hans was there voluntarily. Hans stood out from the others. He had no tattoos, no ear piercings, and he didn't smoke. Was he in the right place? The visit with Hans was very surfacy. The girls were quiet, I was standoffish, and Hans was reserved. We were there for maybe an hour. I felt like such a horrible mom exposing them to such a dark and gloomy situation. Was Hans really getting the help he needed?

Once again, Hans was released from the Regional Mental Health Center earlier than thirty days because of his progress with the program. He spent twenty-one of the thirty days there. When Hans was released, he was sent home with two prescriptions and no other plan than a suggestion for him to check out the Swanson Center for their day program. We went to the Swanson Center and found out that because Hans didn't have health insurance, it was going to cost $300 a week for the program. With no job or insurance, there was no way we could afford the care. After thirty days of being out of the Regional Mental Health Center, he relapsed again.

It was the night of the girls' play performance at school, and Hans must have been drinking all day. He was so sick. I didn't know what to do because I had to be with the girls. I called a friend, who came over and ended up taking Hans to the emergency room. Right before the play started, Hans showed up. Apparently, Hans's prescription drugs were only to be used for detoxing, and if used on a regular basis, they triggered the same part of the brain as alcohol did.

The friends we were staying with had a nanny for their children, and she was a wonderful lady. She was about our age, and she quickly became a friend of mine. We would have conversations daily while cooking dinner in the kitchen. At first, I didn't know if she knew why we were living in the basement, and I didn't offer any information. As time went on, we shared more about our lives. I shared with her about Hans's alcoholism, and she shared with me things that had happened in her life. We prayed for each other, and she quickly became my confidante. She helped me with the girls and was there when I needed someone to talk to. This lady was another huge blessing. She was an angel sent from above.

Our friends had a big deck in the front of their house. I would often sit outside on the front porch praying to God, asking him what the lessons were in all this.

I asked God, "How am I going to make it through?"

The nanny was a lifesaver. She would always take the time to talk with me, share her story, and pray for us.

You are exactly where you are supposed to be. Just breathe.

By November of 2012, we had lived with our friends for over a year . . .

Hans was supposed to come to church after work one Sunday, but he never showed up. He was gone all day into the night. When Hans got mad, he would turn off his phone. I would call endlessly. I felt guilty for my interaction with him. I was just so mad and scared. What was he doing with his life? He was not motivated. Didn't he want to make his life better? I felt like he was another child that I was parenting. What happened to my husband who was so good to me and wanted this family? If Hans would get his life together and get a job to support us, I then could find a job I would be happy with. I just wanted to tell Hans to come home so that he, or especially someone else, would not be tragically affected by his choices. I knew he had been drinking. How could I forgive myself? I was partly to blame for him leaving.

That evening, I knew Hans couldn't have been far away because he didn't have much gas in his car. I just prayed and prayed.

"Please, God, help us."

I got a call around 8:00 p.m. from Hans. He was in the Porter Hospital Emergency Room. Hans tried to park in the hospital parking lot but hit the light pole. He was extracted out of the car to the emergency room. Thank God, he was not out driving and that he hadn't hit someone—that was all I could think of. That was the only call I got from him that evening. I was mad, hurt, scared, and in disbelief that this was happening to me and the girls.

I called our pastor, and he made a few phone calls to let me know Hans was taken in for an OWI (operating while intoxicated). This was a Sunday night, and Hans had to wait until Monday to hear his bond. I was in shock. What were we going to do? I only could talk to Hans for two minutes when he called. We had no money, and the bail was set for three thousand dollars. With the help of a friend and my most recent paycheck, I went to post bail—something I didn't have the stomach to do by myself. I was to pick him up at the Porter County Jail. He was court-ordered to take Antabuse three times a week. His license was revoked for six months, plus he had to do community service work. This was all for his first offense of an OWI.

Whom would we call to help us? Hans needed an attorney. We had never had to deal with something like this before. What on earth? Hans called a friend who was a defense attorney. This friend, his wife, and their family attended our church. Hans knew him from when he coached his son's soccer team, and I knew his wife from the Boys & Girls Clubs. They were a very Christian family who we trusted and loved. This friend knew the formality of the OWI process. It was pretty standard and exactly what he told Hans it was going to be. Was this finally rock bottom? Had Hans finally learned that he was going down the wrong path?

Christmas 2012

Christmas caroling 2012

Making gingerbread houses 2012

Over the next six months, I took him for his Antabuse appointments three times a week, dropped him at work, and picked him up. I took him to AA meetings. I so badly wanted Hans to get better. It was a lot of extra work, but at the time, it was worth it because Hans was working on his sobriety, and I so much wanted him to get better. Our family life seemed to be getting back on track. Was this finally the answer?

After a year and a half of living in our friends' basement and six months of sobriety for Hans, we felt it was time to finally get our own place again. It could only get better from there. We had been through the valley of darkness, and we were finally seeing the light of a new beginning for our family.

Never forget three different types of people who come into your life:
Those who helped you in your most difficult times.
Those who left you in your most difficult times.
Those who put you in difficult times.

* * *

March 2013

Lisa Scheller was tagged.

Hannah Scheller added a new photo to the album: **SPRING BREAK 2013** — with **Delaney Scheller** and **Lisa Scheller**.

March 23, 2013 ·

SPRING BREAK 2013-Minnesota Here We Come!

Girls going to Minnesota Spring Break 2013

Hans

He who has a why to live for can bear almost any how.
—*Friedrich Nietzsche*

Alcoholics do not have relationships; they take hostages. My immediate hostages were Lisa and my daughters. Lisa was dealing with some issues of her own—such as codependency, in which she did not hold me accountable for my actions and, to a certain extent, allowed my behavior to continue, of which I took complete advantage. This is one of the worst things for an alcoholic. In most instances, we will not change unless we have to. We have so many triggers to drinking that I almost believed just breathing might be a trigger for me. However, there are also triggers to recovery. It can be a person (such as a spouse, child, parent, significant other, or close friend), religion, or helping others—anything that makes you want to not only live but thrive. Every alcoholic who has some recovery time has a why, a purpose.

My wife and daughters received the brunt of my alcoholism. As someone who was supposed to be an example and a positive, supportive part of their lives, I was there physically most of the time yet rarely there emotionally. I confused and disappointed them with my neglect, and what made it worse was that they saw who I could be on my rare checked-in days. I loved them no less then than I do now even though I did not have the capability to show it at the time. They knew how much I loved them but must have thought that I hated them at the same time because of my behavior. I was so focused on my addiction and sustaining it that they seemed to live on the periphery of my life. They have always been the why in my life, but I did not have the sobriety skills to use that to my advantage.

One of the worst feelings that a man can have is knowing that they put their children's safety in jeopardy by drinking and driving with them in the car. I was drinking so much that I knew I had to give up either drinking so much or driving. I gave up neither. Thank God that nothing horrible happened during those times.

The worst instance was when I had the girls in the car, but I had not had a lot to drink that day. We needed to go shopping at the grocery store, so I thought that I needed to have something before we went. I chugged some vodka, and off we went. During the drive, I started to feel the effects, and by the time we arrived at the grocery store, I had a hard time getting out of the car. I told the girls that I just needed to sit for a minute, but they knew what was going on, and when they could not reach Lisa, they called a friend to come and get them. By that time, someone else had called the police, who arrived and saw what was happening. The friend took the girls home, and the police took me to the hospital to be tested. I had blood drawn and was at a BAC of .19.

I knew that I was in trouble, so when the nurse and officer left the room, I got up and walked out of the hospital without anyone stopping me. There should have been serious consequences for what I did, but nothing happened, which reinforced that I believed I could handle anything and get away with it. There were so many things that I did that I only understood the significance of when I became sober. It is hard for someone who thinks that they are doing fine but are actually only self-absorbed and not willing to admit their issues. It's said that one of the best things that sobriety brings is getting your feelings back. Getting your feelings back is also one of the worst things about sobriety. When I drove drunk with the girls, I did not really think about it one way or another. I just did it. As I look back now and see the ramifications of what could have happened, I feel devastated. The addiction overrides everything in your life. It is the first and foremost thing that needs to be satisfied each and every single day and leaves little time or desire to do the right thing.

At the church we started attending, I met the head pastor, Pastor Wayne, who had experience working with alcoholics in his past. He became sort of a father figure to me and gave sermons that were very relatable to real life. Lisa and I also met another family who had dealt with similar issues and had two young daughters and became our friends as they both could help us understand and try to comprehend what was happening to us and deal with it.

One December morning, after I took Lisa to work and I was driving home, I was careless, and the car skidded on some ice on a back road while going over a small hill. I had been reaching for a bottle that I had hidden under the seat. The car went into the ditch, overturned, and ended up in the front yard of a house. While collecting my thoughts, I realized that I was wet all over. I expected to find blood when I touched my face, but it was just water from the road and yard. I was not hurt, and the car ended on its wheels, so I had time to take the bottle and hide it in the branches of a pine tree, and I hoped no one would see it. The homeowner came out to see if I was okay. I called Lisa to tell her, and she called the police to notify them. When they came and saw that I was all right, they called a tow truck, and I called my friend to come pick me up. No one found the bottle. As a matter of fact, one of my main concerns was when I would be able to come back for it and not the loss of our vehicle, and I was thankful that I hit a pine tree because the branches would obscure my bottle even in the winter.

Things had gotten so bad that Lisa had talked to numerous people about my situation, and the consensus was that I needed serious help. There was another recovery facility called Regional Mental Health close by that focused not only on detox and short-term care but also on thirty days of recovery. Lisa was able to find me a bed there, and when I spoke to the intake person on the phone, he told me to come in the next day, but I was not supposed to stop drinking in the meantime. This puzzled me until he replied when I asked him that if I stopped completely before I checked in the next day, I could die from withdrawal. This was what my life had come to.

> *Be kind, for everyone you meet is fighting a hard battle.*
> —*Socrates*

It was March 2012. The second rehab was much different from my first one. I was starting to realize the magnitude of what I needed to overcome. This was where I actually took step 1 of AA. I was powerless over alcohol, and my life was definitely unmanageable. Now what do I do with it? I learned many things during those thirty days, and some of them were actually beneficial. The first two days were spent going through monitored withdrawal. Not only does your body react physically with vomiting, cold sweats, hallucinations, and seizures, but also the emotional aspect of it involved, wanting to die from the unbearable thoughts racing through your head—thoughts of regret, shame, hopelessness, and utter defeat. The days that followed consisted of a set schedule of eating, classes, counseling, recreation, and socialization. During the socialization time, I realized that probably less than half of the patients there were attempting a serious recovery from addiction. The others consisted of people who were court-mandated to avoid jail or just wanted some downtime to get their lives back together but knew that they were going to use or drink when they were released. There were some patients who were past recovery. Their mental functions had decreased to a point where it seemed they could not even make decisions pertaining to their own lives. Some patients were there hiding from the police because the police could not remove them from the facility.

One patient told a story that was hard to fathom. He recalled a party he went to in the summer at a friend's house where he woke up the next morning with his sheets completely bloody. Having no recall of what had happened, he asked a friend, who told him that he had said that he had missed winter and snow, so he was going to pretend that it was winter. He lay down in the driveway made of sharp stones and proceeded to try to make numerous "gravel angels" while only wearing shorts. His most successful way to hide the alcohol was in a two-gallon gasoline container. The difference between him and most alcoholics was that he was not trying to hide it so his family wouldn't pour it out; he was hiding it to keep the rest of his family members from finding it and drinking it themselves. This was his life and what he was going to be going back to. At that point, it sank in that I had support from my wife and friends, and I saw a glimmer of hope that I could recover.

The rest of the time in the facility had its ups and downs. While many of the patients looked at it as only a brief sober vacation, some tried their hardest at getting the tools to stay sober once released. It was there that I heard one of the most important tenets of AA. "People, places, and things" describes that in recovery, you *must* avoid certain people.

"People" are generally your old drinking buddies, family, or friends who think that you may be just going through a phase or will get it together soon and be able to party with them like before. There is nothing wrong with those people, and every alcoholic would love to be a person who can drink in moderation and know when to stop. We are not conditioned to be able to drink in moderation.

"Places" are reminders of where constant alcohol consumption happened, such as bars, camping, sporting events, and anything else that alcohol was mandatory for me in order to participate. Attending concerts and watching sporting events always involved alcohol for me.

Some "things" could be almost anything that triggers a visceral reaction. I love pizza, but I do not think I had a slice of pizza without a beer to wash it down for about forty years, and I ate a lot of pizza.

Recovery does not happen all at one time. You need to build a solid foundation upon which your sobriety rests. It includes AA meetings, your higher power, following the twelve steps, and avoiding certain people, places, and things. Oscar Wilde said, "Every saint has a past, and every sinner has a future." Our relapses should not inspire guilt but perseverance. Always remember that feeling guilty means that somewhere inside of you there is still the desire to be sober whether you realize it or not. Take pride in moving forward and take solace that no one does recovery perfectly, and experience is gained if you do relapse. I believe that the larger the trials are that are presented to someone, the larger capacity for tremendous things to result from it. As a soccer coach, I felt that some of my success was from the fact that as I was instructing the players, I could also show them exactly what I wanted because I had been there. I was a soccer player also and did not just read about it.

One thing that rehab does not do very well is prepare you for confronting the same obstacles that you had when you went in. It cannot replicate in a sterile setting actually having to make the decisions that free will provides. Avoiding people, places, and things is important, but the actual change needs to come from within. Nobody should ever think that an inpatient treatment center will "cure" you. What it will do, however, is prepare you with some tools to fight the addiction when you are back in society. It is up to the addict to formulate a plan to utilize these tools, wisdom, and inner fortitude. Decisions and sacrifices must be made in order to stay sober.

One problem that I always had was that I thought that I was the exception to the rule. Telling myself "I can quit any time I want—I've done it a hundred times" actually made sense to me. The rule of drinking in moderation or easily quitting does not work for most alcoholics. I tried drinking only beer, only at night, only with food, only on weekends, only with other people, and the only thing I accomplished was drinking only on days ending with a *y*.

Shortly after coming back from rehab, I went to the Indiana Dunes Great Banquet for the first time. It is a three-day retreat with Christ-based fellowship, teaching, and testimonies about God and overcoming hardships. It, as with most things, helped me but could not, by itself, keep me from drinking. At the retreat, I heard testimonies from many men who had encountered trials in their lives and how they overcame them. It was another step forward in recovery; it was a positive in my life that I could reflect on.

I had a part-time job working for a food distributor, which ended on a Sunday morning in the late fall of 2012. I had a job and had some short-term sobriety. I was able to buy my own car and had a job interview that went so well I was going to start the job on Monday morning. Things were looking up for me.

After finishing my route at 9:00 a.m., I was supposed to meet my family at church for service, but instead, I started drinking in my car. Church suddenly lost its appeal, and I just started driving. The next thing that I knew, a bright light was shining in my face. Confusion led the way to the realization that my face and head hurt badly, and I wondered to myself if I had an accident or, God forbid, had hurt or killed someone.

Apparently, I was driving and went to park in a parking lot when I hit a light standard and blacked out. The parking lot was at the local county hospital, and had it happened in a more remote location, my injuries would have been a lot worse as I was bleeding badly. I believe it was another instance of God looking out for me even when I could not.

The pain I woke to was a nurse and doctor cleaning up the blood on my face and scalp as well as removing hundreds of slivers of glass when my face went through the windshield. I was still in the driver's seat when police found me, and my blood alcohol level was almost 0.3, so they charged me with a class A misdemeanor, suspended my license for six months, and ordered mandatory substance abuse classes, community service, Antabuse for six months, and a year of probation. Antabuse is a powerful drug that makes you violently ill if you consume alcohol while on it.

During my six months on Antabuse, I did not drink, and my emotional state ranged from happy to sad almost on a daily basis. This happened in the fall, so Lisa had to get up with me three times per week at 5:00 a.m. to take me to the health department. It was about fifteen miles, and the weather was bad most of the time. I completed the program and got my license back and was on probation for a year.

I had gone to some AA classes but didn't understand that just attending and not applying the principles did nothing. You don't get sober through osmosis. Some of the excuses at meetings even amazed me, and I was not very understanding of other people's failures because I could not understand my own. I learned some things at the classes, but the addiction was with me 24-7, and that was much more powerful than even daily meetings and counseling.

I was one day short of having one year of sobriety when I attended a golf outing and walked through the clubhouse to the bathroom. Because it was about 8:00 a.m., the bar was closed, but I still grabbed a bottle of vodka and chugged about half of it on my way back to the course. I then went on with my day as though nothing had happened. In fifteen seconds, a year of sobriety was lost. I have no idea why I did it, and there was no craving ahead of time.

At a later AA meeting, I heard that you actually relapse in your mind even before you have the first drink. Once your mind crosses the threshold and allows you to think even for a second that it will be different this time, you have started to relapse. It does not mean that you will pick up a drink, but it has become a possibility. If you are aware of what can happen next, you can avoid relapse. Little by little, I was understanding the magnitude of what got ahold of me, and I was pretty sure that I could do nothing about it.

A man's best friend

Covington

Lisa

*Our job is not to judge. Our job is not to figure out if
someone is deserving. Our job is to lift those who have fallen,
to restore the broken, and to try to heal the hurting.*

I n April of 2013, after a year and a half of living in our friends'
basement, we decided it was finally time to find our own
place again. I was pretty sure Hans had hit his rock bottom
with his OWI and things could only get better. Hans had been
sober for six months, and it was time to put our past behind us
and move forward as a family. I read that an alcoholic needed
to be sober for at least six months for their brain to heal and to
start thinking differently. Hans had been going to AA meetings
three times a week and was working. The girls were doing great
in school, and I liked my job. I was big on making sure the girls
knew everyone had to do their part.

Hans and I found a nice house to rent in a small subdivision
with the possibility to buy. It was the perfect size, had plenty of
room for everyone, and the landlord let us keep Polly. We gathered
our friends to help us move all our personal belongings out of our
four storage units. It felt like Christmas because we had not seen
a lot of our things for over a year. The girls were excited to have
their own rooms, and I was over the top that we finally had our
own place again.

We moved in around mid-April, right before Hannah's
thirteenth birthday. The first weekend in May, I was ready to

attend the Indiana Dunes Great Banquet women's weekend. Though things had improved considerably, I still didn't feel one-hundred-percent confident leaving the girls home alone with Hans. However, many friends assured me that I didn't need to worry about Hans or the girls and they would make sure to keep an eye on things at the house. They encouraged me to attend the women's weekend and take time for myself. I told myself the camp was just two miles down the road and if there was an emergency, I wouldn't be too far away. I got to camp, and I really was nervous about the unknown. I didn't feel like I could relax.

As the weekend went on, I started to feel more comfortable and knew this was where I needed to be. The love I felt and the outpouring of support from others was unbelievable. What an amazing spiritual weekend that really deepened my faith as well as my belief in the Holy Spirit, Jesus, and God. I came home on Sunday feeling renewed, strengthened, and blessed by my many new Christian sisters. I was so thankful for all that God had done in my life and our families.

First night at Covington

Hans had already been to the men's weekend, and I believed if he got out of his weekend what I got out of my weekend, we were definitely headed on the right path with God by our side. We were no longer in a hopeless situation. We had a new community of brothers and sisters in Christ, and our future looked so much brighter.

Our family continued to go to the Presbyterian Church. We really enjoyed our friends, the fellowship, and being involved. We did a lot of giving back with the men's shelter, youth group, and any other way we could, which made us feel good.

Pastor Wayne ended up retiring due to his health and moved to Michigan with his wife. It was a tough time for the congregation as well as for Hans and me. I was very concerned about Hans because he had developed a strong relationship with our pastor. It was like a father-son relationship. Hans trusted the pastor, could talk to him easily, and really enjoyed his sermons and the support. The church hired an interim pastor, whom we got to know, but the relationship that developed wasn't quite the same. What was Hans going to do without his friend?

Summer came, and Hannah attended her first mission trip with members of our church. The girls also went to visit my dad in Minnesota for a couple of weeks. They called it "Papa's Camp on the Farm." The girls got to spend time with their cousins—boating, riding four-wheelers, and so much more. I was so blessed that they had this opportunity and that my dad was willing to have them. Hans was working part-time jobs, refinishing furniture, attending meetings, and searching for a full-time job. I still worried about Hans. I kept tabs on him. I was a helicopter wife. I felt I needed to know where he was going, what he was spending his money on, and see if I could find signs of him drinking again. I didn't feel like I could totally trust him.

Hannah's first mission trip

Maybe you are the lighthouse in someone else's storm.

In the fall, Hannah started eighth grade at Chesterton Middle School, and Delaney started sixth in Discovery Charter School. One of Hannah's good friends lived in the subdivision next to us. Hannah rode the bus with her friend to school, and Hans or I would take Delaney to school. It was very important to keep the girls' lives consistent. They had lots of good, stable friends. Hans was starting to reach out to more friends and make more connections. He also served on the fall men's banquet team. I was always so thankful when he did things with other guys as it took a burden off me.

I was relieved when Hans started taking the initiative on his job search, but I was also apprehensive because of the choices he had made in his past that might affect him getting a stable job. He had interviewed for a couple of jobs he would have absolutely loved; he got really excited about the interviews and felt confident he was going to be hired. I wasn't one-hundred-percent confident and questioned him a lot, knowing the red flags that would come up when they did a background check.

I could sense Hans was not taking it well. I was worried about him feeling hopeless and relapsing. I knew Hans wanted so badly to put his past behind him and take care of his family. I tried to keep his spirits up and remind him that maybe the particular job was not in God's plan. Something better was going to come along. We needed to keep doing the next right thing.

As with each job denial, the stress level and anxiety increased. Hans would tell me he was fine, but I knew deep down he was not. I truly believed, if Hans got a stable job, then I could start doing the things I wanted to do. Was it my nature to take care of everything, or was it a feeling that my life was unstable and I needed to be in control?

The girls were always reminded since they were in elementary school how important it was for everyone in the family to do their part. I would tell the girls that it was their job to go to school and get good grades and it was Mom and Dad's job to go to work. When Hans wasn't working, it was hard to justify all this to the girls.

Lisa Scheller
December 14, 2013

These are my girls out visiting the Ronald McDonald House in Chicago today with their youth group! Great job!

Hannah Scheller is with Delaney Scheller and 7 others.
December 14, 2013 · Burns Harbor
Fun day with the youth group in Chicago!

Ronald McDonald House Giveback

In January 2014, we experienced a bad snowstorm. All four of us were stuck at home for three weeks—two for Christmas break and one for a snow blizzard. Things got really edgy. The girls were antsy. Hans was bored with no work, and I was working plus taking on additional projects to make extra money.

Signs of Hans's behavior started to become very strange and unpredictable again. He was displaying very negative and sarcastic behavior. He wanted to sleep all the time and not be engaged with the family. I had a sense he had relapsed but wasn't one-hundred-percent sure. I would ask him if he had been drinking, and he would get very defensive and say no.

I learned the signs of Hans drinking. He would get annoyed quickly. He was defensive and sarcastic. His eyes were glossed over. He had a twitch in his face and a stale smell. We would get into a fight. He would start calling me nasty names and leave. Yes, I was bitchy. I was mad about him not fulfilling his obligations to his family, and the only way for him to deal with things was to drink.

I was a madwoman when I knew Hans was drinking and he told me that he wasn't. When he lied to me, I became outraged, and I searched everywhere for the alcohol. I was determined to find the bottles and prove myself right. Sometimes I found them, and sometimes I didn't. Finding the bottles made me livid.

The tabs I felt I needed to keep on Hans were psychotic. I became immersed in micromanaging him. I kept track of all he was doing. I made him call me when he got to where he was going and when he was leaving places. I wanted to hear his voice so that I could tell if he was drinking. I got really good at recognizing his drinking voice. There was a time he told me he was going to an AA meeting, and I trusted him. I so badly wanted to trust him and not micromanage him. Thirty minutes after he left, I heard someone at the door. Thank God, the girls were not home. I answered the door, and it was a police officer.

My heart sank, and he said, "Are you Hans Scheller's wife?"

I said, "Yes."

He said, "We got a phone call from a neighbor."

I thought to myself, *What the heck? Now what?*

Hans didn't go to the AA meeting as he had told me. He went down the road, parked his car, and was drinking. The police officer drove me to him, and sure enough, he was blitzed. The police officer was so kind and told me that I could drive him home. Right there, the police officer could have charged him with an OWI. I was beyond mad but still thankful.

Things started to become very shaky again. Hans hid his alcohol from me as much as he could. I found bottles under couches, on top of cabinets, in the trunk of our car by the spare tire, between the mattresses, in the dresser, among his clothes, in the furnace room, and under the deck. Some were thrown in the trees by where we lived. There was a period where he drank a lot of Gatorade and was drinking his vodka in it. He would hide his vodka in water bottles. I sniffed a number of water bottles because I knew he had been drinking. Where was he getting all the money for the alcohol? I was the one who knew where every penny in our house went. We sometimes did not have money for food, but he found money for alcohol.

One day I was cleaning our master bedroom closet and found money hidden among Hans's sweaters. Where was he getting the money? We had no extra money. I confronted Hans and asked him about the money.

"What? I am not doing anything," he would say, or "I don't know what you are talking about." Or he would make up some excuse. It finally came out that Hans was selling off his album collection to the record shop to support his addiction.

What the heck?

He could sell his albums for alcohol but not for food on the table. When I was stressing about how we were going to pay the bills, he was stressing about where the money would come from for his alcohol. The trust was broken once again. I was livid and so beside myself about what to do. I tried to keep positive but was exhausted from the roller-coaster ride we were on. My main priority was the girls—their safety and them living a close-to-normal life, whatever that normal was. At this point, we had so many friends that knew of our family situation that they were very supportive of the girls and me.

Easter 2014

Picture from Hannah to brighten Lisa's day

It was April 2014, and after another week of binge-drinking (which I knew about), Hans was very sick. He didn't hide how sick he was and told the girls and me he had the flu. I knew darn well it wasn't the flu, but . . . my goal was to get him to bed. Our room was in the basement. I went between checking on Hans and taking care of the girls.

When is this ever going to stop?

The next morning Hannah had gone to school, and I had just dropped Delaney off at school when I got a phone call from a friend saying, "Do you know where Hans is?"

I said, "Yes, he is at home. Why?"

"Are you sure?" she asked.

"Yes," I said.

"His friend had just got a strange call from him, thanking him for his friendship, and we believe he is trying to commit suicide."

What?

My mind and heart were racing. This couldn't be happening. Thank God, the girls were at school.

What is he doing? God, please help me deal with whatever I go home to.

I didn't even know if Hans was at home or if he left. The mile drive seemed like an hour. I drove into the subdivision and got to our driveway. His car was still there. I ran into the house. Polly did not come to meet me as she usually did. I went down to our bedroom, and there was Hans in bed. I didn't know if he was dead or just passed out. I thought he was fine when I left to bring Delaney to school. I went closer to him and saw a bottle of my prescription and a note.

The note read:

> Lisa I am sorry. I love you and the girls a lot and you do not deserve this. Wishing you the best.
> Love, Hans.

My God.

"How many did you take?" I asked.

He was unconscious with no response. I called his name, and he didn't reply. I shook him, and he murmured. I had no idea how many pills he took and if he was drinking with the pills. I immediately called 911. The ambulance and police arrived within minutes. I was so scared. The police officer and paramedics were talking to Hans. The police officer asked Hans what the heck he was doing. They brought in the stretcher, and they took him to the hospital and ended up pumping his stomach. They asked if I wanted to ride with them, and I said no. I was in disbelief. My adrenaline was racing, and I couldn't think straight. I called my sister. I called the pastor, and I called my good friend. The pastor told me she would go visit Hans at the hospital.

Sometimes the bad things that happen in our lives put us directly on the path to the best things that will ever happen to us.

My friend from church came over immediately. As always, she just listened. She hugged me, and not once did she tell me what I needed to do or pass judgment. My friend found out from her husband where Hans hid his empty bottles. Once again I was blindsided by the extent of Hans's drinking. I had an inkling he had been drinking, but I wanted so bad to trust him. I wanted the disease to go away and stop haunting our family. The girls didn't ask for this to be their life.

My friend asked if I had some garbage bags because she was going to get rid of the empty bottles. She was always so good to me. I sat upstairs while I heard her tossing bottles into not just one garbage bag but seven or eight large garbage bags, if not more.

Oh my gosh, how could I have been so blind?

She took the garbage bags filled with empties and got rid of them. Once again I was so grateful to have my friend. I was so thankful the girls were at school. And I was so thankful Hans was alive.

My friend left and I went to the hospital to meet the interim pastor. I didn't want to see Hans by myself. I was so mad and disappointed. They had Hans in a suicide watch section of the hospital. The pastor and I went to his room. The pastor did all the talking. I couldn't say anything. Hans said he wanted to take his life because he did not want to live like this anymore. He was ashamed of his life and could not see it getting better. The pastor told him, it was not his choice to take his life. After about a fifteen-minute visit, we left the hospital.

That day the girls came home from school, and I sat them down to tell them about their dad.

Hannah's first response to me (she was in eighth grade) was, "Don't sugarcoat it, Mom. Dad has alcohol poisoning. We have been learning about this at school in health class."

I sat and looked at her, trying to not overreact.

"Mom, I knew he had alcohol poisoning last night when he was violently sick. If he doesn't stop drinking, he could die."

Hannah was absolutely right. I didn't want to appear like I was shocked that she knew this. This was now about sharing the truth with the girls that Dad was ill and his disease had flared up.

Hans stayed in the hospital under a seventy-two-hour watch, and the doctors decided because of his suicide attempt, he should go to Porter Starke Inpatient Care for a couple of days. I reached out to Hans's attorney friend to tell him where Hans was at. I was so thankful that our attorney friend took the time to go visit with Hans. I was a broken record—what I said to Hans was nagging, lecturing, or nonsense to him. Hans wanted to hear nothing from me and tuned me out. I didn't go and visit Hans at Porter Starke for a couple of days. I told the girls their dad was in the hospital again, getting help for his disease. Pretty much he was being detoxed once again.

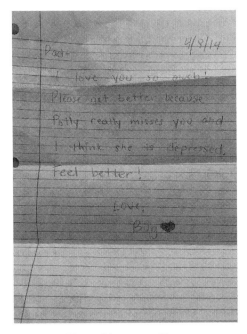

Hannah's note to Hans

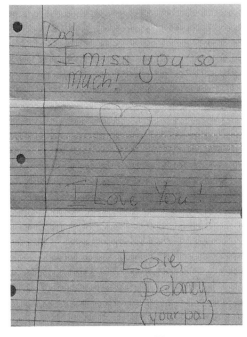

Laney's note to Hans

The day Hans was going to be released from Porter Starke, I did go see him. Hans and I met with the doctor about what the plans should be when he was released. Hans had alcohol-induced depression, the doctor said. It totally made sense. Alcohol made Hans depressed, and he drank more, which put him in a darker place. The doctor gave him medication for depression and recommended Hans see a psychiatrist and do an outpatient program.

During this time, the pastor shared with me the book *Codependence: The Dance of the Wounded Souls.* I devoured the book and could totally relate to its messages. One of the statements that spoke clearly to me was, "We are spiritual beings having a human experience." After reading this, I firmly believed it. We are all some sort of spirit that was created in a body. God knows the plan he has for us and what our experiences are going to be.

Hans did not have health insurance, and we didn't know how we were going to pay for all these new medical bills. Hans and I made an appointment with the outpatient center. The intake person explained to us that they recommended Hans be part of a program that was every day for four hours for twelve weeks. The cost without insurance was $400 weekly, and there was not any financial assistance because I made above the income guideline.

Four hundred dollars a week—how would we afford that?

I just couldn't understand how an income of less than $40,000 was to support a family of four. We were already in a bankruptcy. We couldn't get a loan; we had no disposable income; and there was no way we could afford an additional $1,600 per month on my salary. Over time we always heard the best prescription for alcoholism was ninety days of AA. Every day for ninety days. We could afford this. It was free, and Hans could continue to take his antidepressant. We had no choice but to go in this direction.

In May of 2014, our landlord decided she wanted to put the house we were renting on the market. We were definitely not in the position to buy it. She wanted me to make sure it was ready for showings and let the house be shown when the realtor called. I was juggling a lot that I didn't have time to be keeping a house clean for showings. We did it for a while, but then she decided it would be better empty, so she gave us a thirty-day notice. Where were we going to go now?

Girls going to see Papa in Minnesota

* * *

Hans

In the spring of 2013, I had about six months of sobriety, and we were able to save enough money to rent a house and move out of our friends' basement, so things were going in a positive manner. One misconception about alcoholism is, you are more likely to relapse when your life takes a downturn. It could happen just as easily when you were doing well and got caught off guard. It might be just wanting to celebrate your good fortune or, as in my case so many times, thinking that you could control it.

I cannot drink like other people and never will be able to. That is just fine. Everyone is different, with a variety of strengths and weaknesses, yet everyone is perfect in God's eyes.

Needless to say, the sobriety did not last. I went to AA meetings and celebrated my sobriety by drinking on the way home numerous times—very crazy.

Shortly after moving, our car started to have problems, and we took it to a local repair shop. Our transmission needed to be replaced, and they quoted us $1,200. While that amount hurt our bank account, we knew that we had to do it or buy another car, which we could not afford either. The repair shop kept coming up with different numbers after that. Soon the transmission on a car valued at about $3,500 was going to cost us $3,000. I thought, *Here we go again!*

We socialized with some of our church friends, including a day trip to St. Joseph, Michigan, to go to the beach, shop, and have dinner. There were actually a lot of fun times that we had together.

During this time, I kept procrastinating going to the sheriff's department to pay a $200 fine that I owed. I never seemed to have the money available to do that while I always found money for alcohol. A friend bought our used water softener for $200, and I thought that I would use that to pay my debt. A few days went by, and I did not pay it, and in my warped way of thinking, I believed that nothing would actually happen. There was no urgency to do the right thing even though it would have been very easy to do so. One evening after dinner, there was a knock on the door, and we ignored it as we usually did. After a few minutes, someone yelled, "Police, open the door." We decided to hide in the basement and hope that they went away, but they did not. They told me that because I did not pay the

$200, they were taking me to jail until it was paid. They handcuffed me in front of the neighbors, put me in the squad car, and took me away. Incredulously, I did not let them know that I had the money at the house or bother to take it with me to pay the debt.

A friend of mine had an AA phrase of "stinking thinking," which was where I was at. A different friend brought the money to jail because Lisa couldn't bring herself to do it. In the jail, they told me that if I had answered the door and told them that I had the money, I could have followed them to jail and paid it, and it would have been over.

Two weeks later, I was coming home and parked in our subdivision a few houses away from mine so I could have a drink before getting home. I told Lisa I was going to an AA meeting but only drove around. After a while, a police car pulled in behind me on the street, came up to my car, and asked me what I was doing. He smelled alcohol on my breath and saw the top of a bottle poking out from beneath the front seat. Because I was only a short distance from home, he said that he would get Lisa and bring her to my car and have her drive me home. Once again, the girls saw a police officer at the house having an issue with me. As ashamed as I was, my main thoughts were that I was ecstatic that he did not find the other full bottle that I had under the other seat. I felt that I had pulled one over on him.

Alcohol was consuming me, and my family was the collateral damage. I did not realize it, but I was actually holding myself prisoner. Without rational thought, there would be no recovery, and while I was drinking, there would be no rational thought. It was a vicious cycle that I did not know how to break.

Hans's AA coins

I applied for many jobs over that winter that I thought I was qualified for, but after some very good interviews and showing a lot of interest, they all said no after doing my background checks. I was becoming very disillusioned, and the instability was affecting me negatively from an emotional standpoint.

I had finally gotten a job doing sales on commission for a local water park, and it was difficult and not very profitable with a lot of rejection. This dark period was when suicide crossed my mind for the first time. I started to think about it more and actually weighed the pros and cons. Saying that I rationally considered suicide is an oxymoron of epic proportions, but that was what I thought I was doing. You cannot be rational if you are thinking of doing something that destructive.

One morning, in April 2014, after Lisa and I had another fight, I thought that it was time. She left for a day of appointments for her job, and I grabbed my bottle and a bottle of pain medication. I put the pills in my mouth and washed them down with the vodka. I sent a few texts, wrote a note for Lisa, and lay on the bed and closed my eyes.

As it turned out, Lisa came back home shortly after she left, which she never did. She found me with the vodka and empty pill bottle on the nightstand and could barely wake me. Only about thirty minutes in total had gone by before the paramedics started to work on me. They were able to resuscitate me, and I spent the next three days at the hospital on suicide alert. A sheriff's officer came to escort me to the local mental health center. It turned out that it was a former player of mine at Valparaiso High School. He told me that it was mandatory that he handcuffed patients he transported on suicide watch but that he could not do that to me—a small measure of grace. To this day, I still get choked up when I think about this small gesture that allowed me to keep what little respect for myself that I had. Sobriety does not come all at once; it comes in small doses that allow you to pull yourself up a little at a time.

The two days I was at the mental health center were spent eagerly waiting to be released, yet I didn't know what waited for me when I would leave. The nurse who checked on me was the wife of a friend of mine, and I felt embarrassed, but she showed me only compassion. Lisa made some phone calls to ensure that I still had a job when I was released.

As I took time to think about what I had tried to do, the enormity of it was hard to comprehend. If I had succeeded, that was it. No do-overs. No going back. All the lives I had touched would have gotten a figurative slap in the face. It would be not only giving up on myself but giving up on everyone who cared for me. My death would not have benefitted a single person and especially not my family. No matter how miserable and unhappy I was, no one deserved to have to deal with that. I know that a lot of people sometimes feel that there is no other way out.

Three people came to see me after my suicide attempt. Ken and his wife were friends from church who show love and compassion to everyone. The other person—while being in the forefront in parts of my life and in the background in others—had always had a major impact on my life. Gary had seen all phases of my life from being suicidal, an inmate, a loving father, and a brother in Christ. He sat beside me as I contemplated what I thought was the emptiness of my life and my future. He was my friend during good times, my lawyer during incarceration, and my inspiration at all times.

Christian band

Sometimes when people say or do something, it can have long-term ramifications. It can be positive or negative. Those three people visiting me were a few more handholds on my climb up. I wanted to stop but did not have the tools to do it. I was confused with no clear picture of everything that real sobriety looked like since it had been so many years that I lived a completely sober life. I could not afford the IOP, or intensive outpatient program, for treatment that was recommended, so I tried again to do it on my own with predictable results.

Summer after Covington

Lisa

God is good all the time. All the time God is GOOD!

O n July 1, we moved all our things back into storage and rented a cottage in New Buffalo for a couple of weeks. It felt like we were on vacation! While there, we celebrated our fourteenth wedding anniversary and Delaney's eleventh birthday. We loved New Buffalo. Hans and I could continue to work while at the cottage and save some money. We also started searching for a new place to live, but many would not take dogs. There was no way we were not going to bring Polly with us. Polly was a loyal family companion, especially to Hans.

After the two weeks, we headed back to the Valparaiso area and stayed in a couple of different hotels; the vacation continued, but the hotel living got old. The girls were troopers, and we tried to keep things as normal as possible and fun. When I was worried or scared, I needed to remind myself that Jesus had the wheel and would meet every one of our needs. At this point, we were pretty much homeless. We really had nowhere to go, and our future was unknown. This was not a way to raise the girls.

I finally said to Hans, "I am taking the girls and Polly to Minnesota to see my dad."

We had a month before school started. Hans said he would find a friend to live with and continue working. The girls loved going to Papa's, and my dad had always told me the doors were always open. I needed time to process everything. The girls and

I left Valparaiso with Polly and headed north. I was not feeling one-hundred-percent certain that Hans was going to be okay, but my heart was telling me I had no choice. I needed the girls to be in a safe and fun environment. We said goodbye to Hans, and he assured me not to worry.

New Buffalo, 2014

The girls and I made it to Minnesota, and what a relief it was to be with my dad. I did not tell him we were coming until we were four hours away. We arrived on his doorstep at 10:00 p.m., unloaded our car, and no questions were asked. I tried calling Hans along the way, and he was not answering. I got ahold of him at 9:30 p.m., and he was very short with me. I definitely knew he had been drinking.

I didn't realize how exhausted, tired, and overwhelmed I was about life—I thought I had it all together. I was always on autopilot. It was the first time that I truly began to think I needed another life plan . . . another do-over. Hans wasn't going to stop drinking, and I couldn't continue to live like this. Our family's life was shaky, and the harder I tried to make things normal and under control, the harder things became.

My friends would say, "You need to take care of yourself, Lisa, for the girls."

What the heck? How could I take care of myself when my life was falling apart and all I could do was put out the fires?

As our family was going through our stormy days, many of our closest friends started to separate and divorce. It was very hard to see this happen. I questioned myself over and over if I was staying in my marriage for all the wrong reasons. Who would I be on my own with the girls, and could I do it? I tried to listen for the voice to tell me I was better off leaving, but I never heard it. Friends would tell me that I shouldn't invest so much time in the drama, I didn't deserve the stress nor ramifications, and the girls and I deserved better. But deep down, I felt I needed to help Hans.

> *One of the hardest life lessons is letting go.*
> *Whether it's guilt, anger, betrayal, love, or loss,*
> *change is never easy. We want to fight to hold on, and*
> *we fight to let go.*

The next day I tried calling Hans repeatedly, and there was no answer. I tried all day, and once I got ahold of him, the phone conversations were very spotty. Nothing made sense. I was so concerned and afraid but knew there was nothing I could do eight hours away. I did not even know where he was. I called my good friend and told her I was worried about him. Her husband saw Hans's car at a run-down motel in Portage. What on earth was he doing there? Hans was paying night by night to stay there. I called another friend, who called the hotel, to do a wellness check on him. Hans was alive but only living on alcohol. Our friend met with Hans. I could not mentally wrap my mind around or understand what was going on. I panicked, anxiety overcame me, and I cried uncontrollably. I was so blessed to be at my dad's where the girls were preoccupied. What was I going to do? I couldn't leave Hans how he was—or should I? I truly knew I was having a nervous breakdown.

I told my dad I needed to head back home and asked if the girls and Polly could stay while I went back to Valparaiso to straighten things out. I had already reached out to my friend to see if her husband would talk or meet with Hans. Her husband agreed to talk with Hans a couple of times on the phone.

During this time, I left the girls in Minnesota with my dad and drove the eight hours back to Valparaiso. Hans did not know

I was coming back. I did not want to expose the girls to whatever I myself was about to walk into. My friend's husband picked up Hans, and I met them both at a local restaurant.

Hans looked terrible, and I was so blessed to see my friend's husband. He sat and talked with us. Hans was apologetic. He had a lot of shame and regret. The friend shared with us his story and said he was willing to help Hans if he was going to accept his help. I felt a sense of relief. Maybe this time, Hans would get it.

Hans and I spent a couple of nights at a Country Inn and Suites in Valparaiso. Hans went to work for a couple of days, and then we headed to Minnesota to pick up the girls.

While back in Minnesota, Hans and I went to visit Hazelden Betty Ford Center in Chisago City, ten miles from my dad's. We walked the grounds, toured the facility, and learned about their programs. We had a friend that attended Hazelton, and we thought it could be an option for Hans to get the treatment he needed on an outpatient basis. The place was amazing—a place where many people all over the world had attended. I felt very blessed that God was putting this opportunity in our life.

While at my dad's, I applied for a couple of jobs and had interviews. I was pretty excited because maybe this was a new beginning for all of us once again.

Papa and the girls

* * *

Hans

After over a year, the lease was coming up on the house, and we needed to move out as the owner wanted to sell the house. With some money in the bank but no clear plan, we rented a small house in New Buffalo, Minnesota, for a couple of weeks to figure things out. It was like a minivacation until the next chapter of our lives started. We had fun at the beach and seeing all the quaint shops downtown.

We decided that maybe it would be good to move back to Minnesota once again. We decided that Lisa would go back for some job interviews that she had lined up. Meanwhile, I would stay at a local hotel in Valparaiso and finish some sales calls I had for my current job. We hugged, kissed, and said goodbye, but both of us had the strange feeling that this goodbye was different.

The first night after she and the girls left, I got Chinese food and Russian alcohol. I did not go to my sales calls, and after a couple of days of assuring Lisa that I was all right, I stopped answering her calls. About three days later, she was so worried about me that she called a friend, who came to check on me. He came and found me in the hotel in a stupor. At his insistence, we went to a meeting and then went to a restaurant to get something to eat and meet Lisa, who I did not know had arrived back in Valparaiso. I had enough foresight to sit at a table by the bathroom so when I had to throw up, I didn't have to go far. Why Lisa and the girls stayed with me after this, I can't begin to fathom. The love they have for me superseded the wreckage I had made out of our lives.

We stayed at a local hotel for a few days while the girls were still in Minnesota and tried to figure things out once again. Our friends agreed to have us stay there again, only this time we prayed that it would only be a short time. Lisa had a great interview and was offered the job and asked to start immediately. The girls stayed with me while Lisa worked at her new job back in Minnesota. I kept drinking and trying to hide it, but the girls finally called Lisa and said that they could not stand it and were afraid, so Lisa came back, and we were once again back to square one.

Hans *"not feeling well."*

The Basement Again

Lisa

*Surrender to follow Jesus . . . God will bring you through it
with his time and his way!*

Not knowing anything for sure about the jobs in Minnesota, we headed back to Chesterton.

We needed to figure out a temporary living situation that would allow us to keep Polly. We were in limbo but knew for sure we couldn't move to Minnesota without jobs. Back in Chesterton, we were running out of time because the new school year was about to begin. Our housing options were limited. Hans did not want to ask our friends again, but it seemed to be our only option. We reluctantly went to visit, and Hans asked sheepishly if we could stay in their basement for a week to buy us more time. It was not what we wanted to do, and I am sure we overstayed our welcome the first time. Once again, they graciously agreed to let us stay with them again, and once again, we set up home in their basement.

I got a job interview in Minnesota for a company that was five miles from my dad's. I first interviewed by Skype and then was invited for a second interview. I headed to my dad's on Thursday, had the second interview that evening, and was offered the job on Friday. The salary was twice what I was making at my current job. Was this God's plan for our new beginning?

After much discussion, Hans and I decided I would take the job in Minnesota. I would move first, save up some money, and then the girls and Hans would join me. Finally, another new fresh start. Hans was very supportive. He promised he could take care of the girls back in Chesterton and we would meet up on weekends. School had not started yet, and we were hoping to be able to make the move by the beginning of the school year. I left Chesterton and made it to my dad's on Sunday. I was hardly settled in Minnesota when Hannah started calling me continuously.

"Dad is yelling at us."

"He is sleeping."

"Mom, we are scared, please come home."

I thought to myself, *What am I doing? This cannot be God's plan.*

This was the first time I had left them with Hans. It was out of the question to bring the family to my dad's, especially since we did not know how long we would need to stay. What was I supposed to do? I had no choice but to pack my bags in Minnesota and head back to Chesterton once again. All I could think of was that the girls needed stability. They needed to be with their friends, and Hannah wanted so badly to participate in the show choir. I knew that with God's help, we would make it through. Back to the drawing board in Chesterton.

The girls started another year of school. Delaney was in seventh grade, and Hannah was in ninth grade. I continued my job. Hans got a job with a local convenience store, and we tried to keep a positive outlook. Our family's faith was being tested.

One Friday night, Hans was at work, Delaney was at a friend's house, and I had an urge inside telling me that I needed to attend an Al-Anon meeting. Hannah went to babysit for some friends, and I headed to the meeting. During the meeting, I heard one of the other participants say, "There are FOUR Cs. You can't control the disease, you can't cure it, nor did you cause it, but you can 'contribute' to the disease."

Right then, a light went off in my head . . . I could not cure the disease, nor did I cause it, and I definitely could not control it, but what I absolutely was doing was *contributing*. I was contributing by yelling, lecturing, demanding, micromanaging, being a helicopter wife, and being a crazy person. None of this was good for the girls or our family. I needed to stop my part of the nightmare. I was trying so hard to do things my way. How was that working?

That Sunday we were at church, doing a fundraiser for the youth group, and Hans needed to leave and go to work. Hans had been acting out of character, and I sensed he might have been drinking again. There was always this distinct smell, and his eyes were glossed over. At this time, he was supposed to be on Antabuse to prevent him from drinking. Hans left and went to work. The girls and I finished up at church. I had this inkling he had not taken the Antabuse, so after church, I went to his work and brought him his medication. He was acting very differently and refused to take the pill. I then knew he had been drinking. He got off work that evening at 10:00 p.m. and did not come home until after midnight.

Picture from Laney to Lisa

Faith *is about believing you don't know what or how it will happen.* But *you know it will!*

The alcohol continued to take a toll on our family. I tried to control it. I thought I could cure him for our family, but it was destroying the girls and me.

That following day, Monday morning, a fall October day, I heard God whisper, *"Surrender and give it to me. This is between*

Hans and me. Not you and Hans. I will take care of your burdens."
Therefore, I simply surrendered.

I got up with the girls, and when they were getting ready for school, I went out to search his car. I found a half-full bottle of vodka in the trunk and a stash of cash. I was livid. I went back into the house, calmly got the girls ready, and drove them to school while Hans was asleep. I took his keys because I knew he had been drinking. After dropping off the girls, I came home, woke him up, and told him he had to leave.

I told him I'd had enough, and the girls did not deserve what he was continuing to do to his family. I took his car keys and hid them because I did not want him drinking and driving. I was more concerned about the innocent people on the roads than I was about Hans at this point. I went to take a shower, and when I came back, he was gone. I ran outside, and my car was gone. I went back inside and saw he had taken a garbage bag of summer clothes but not his wallet or phone. I drove to the nearby park he would go to sometimes, and there was no sign. I called his friend in case Hans had tried to reach out to him. It was not unusual for Hans to leave for a day or overnight, but this time I had a feeling he was really gone. After I saw the bag of clothes he took, I believed he was headed south with no intention of returning. This time he was really gone.

Hans passed out

All day I was on the phone with my sister, my best friend and Hans's friend. This was the final straw. I had no more to give. I prayed he would not get in an accident and that others would not be hurt by his actions. I went between an array of feelings—sadness because he couldn't bring himself to get better, especially for his girls, and anger because he continued to keep going down that crazy, dead-end path. I was emotionally drained, under constant stress, and uncertain about the future. I just wanted the nightmare to be over.

That evening, around 6:00 p.m., I received a phone call from the state patrol.

They said, "Is this Lisa Scheller?"

"Yes," I said.

"We found your car on Highway 65 down by Scottsburg, Indiana, in the highway median. Do you know who was driving it?"

I said, "Yes, my husband."

He said, "We searched for him, and he was nowhere to be found. We had the dogs out looking for him, but nothing. We opened the trunk, and there were several empty vodka bottles. We are not sure where he went." He said, "Wherever he is, he had to have walked a long distance to any nearby gas station. We checked the local hospitals, and there was no sign of anyone who was unidentified. We do not plan to arrest him. We want to get him help if he is in danger." He continued, "If you hear of anything, please let us know."

What on earth? The car was found but no Hans. Where could he be? Did he hitch a ride? Would his body be found somewhere? I was beside myself. I did not know what I would do if he tried to call me for help.

That evening the girls came home from their after-school activities, and once again, I had to sit them down to tell them their dad left, and this time I truly did not know where he was. I explained he left without his phone or wallet. I told them we needed to give it to God and pray.

"Pray lots. God's got this, and he is taking care of Daddy, and he will take care of us."

Eight days went by, and there was nothing from Hans, and all I did was pray.

"God, I know you got this!"

I knew I was going to have to deal with whatever God sent my way.

* * *

Hans

Not until we are lost do we begin to understand ourselves.
—Henry David Thoreau

At the church that our family attended and that you would hear about more later, there were two pastors. One was a male and a former marine, and the other, a female and definitely not a marine. They complemented each other so well that it would be almost impossible to find someone who could not relate and gravitate to either one of them or the other. While both of them were wonderful human beings, the female pastor exuded a soft outside but very strong inside and had enough compassion for ten people. The male pastor was tough on the outside but incredibly caring and understanding on the inside.

The male pastor became somewhat of a mentor to me and gave me my first real "God" moment. It was at an Easter service after the band had played and the sermon had started that I felt something. It was not a vision but an internal peace where things became aligned in my mind, and Jesus actually became real for me. I have often wondered since then why I kept doing destructive things to myself if I felt that presence. I have since realized that the fight between good and evil is ongoing on a daily basis. That day good won. But on many other days, evil won.

It was at this time that Lisa and I started to fight more. I got angrier, and I drank more. We were back for a second time in our friends' basement, and I began to care less and less—if that was even possible. After one argument, I left and walked to the nearest town that had a bar, which was about four miles away. I drank on the way there, at the bar, and walked home late into the night. It was about twenty degrees out, so I had to walk fast. But apparently, on the way home, I wandered into a field and passed out. White snow, my black jacket, and a full moon allowed a police officer to spot me. I have no idea how long I was in the snow, but he was able to wake me up, and instead of taking me to jail, he just asked me where I lived and took me home. Even with all the hurt I had inflicted on other people and myself, I was still being bombarded with grace. It was very much appreciated, yet I could not, at the time, comprehend the magnitude of it. I voluntarily went back on Antabuse to try to quit, but I could not stick with it for more than a couple of months and started to drink again and pretended that I was still taking the medication. Lisa suspected and confronted me, but I denied it.

I was working at a convenience store at the time, and while I was at work during a busy time, Lisa came in, gave me a pill, and said, "Take the Antabuse."

I was embarrassed beyond words and thought to myself, *This is it. I have to get out of here.*

I literally could not think straight or even begin to understand the magnitude of what I was about to do. I took some of the cash register money at the end of my shift and went home. It only got worse from there. I was a complete mess and could barely function, so when Lisa went to take a shower, I grabbed a few clothes, left my wallet and cell phone, and walked out the door with car keys and some cash. I've always loved Key West and the lifestyle it projects, so I thought that if I was going to go somewhere, it might as well be there. I got in the car, stopped at a liquor store, and then headed south.

Hans Heads South

Lisa

*At some point you just have to let go . . . Let go of what
you thought should happen and begin to live in what is
happening.*

Ten days had gone by, and I'd heard nothing from Hans. I
continued to work, and the girls went to school. They had
their after-school activities, we had our church family, and
I had wonderful support from friends and family. I was thankful
for all the love we'd been shown but also frustrated and confused.
What kind of game was Hans playing, and how could he have
done this to his family? Why was he being so selfish? Was this the
memory he wanted to leave for his girls?

After a while, I started to worry. I called our church pastors,
and the girls and I went to visit with them. They were very
supportive and talked with the girls about how they needed to
believe that their dad was okay. They reassured them they were
surrounded by a loving community of friends at church.

At this time, our family was very involved in the church.
I was on the church session as well as the New Pastor Search
Committee. After Hans had been gone for a week, I was at church,
talking to the interim pastor off to the side. She asked me how it
was going. I told her that we had not heard from Hans and that I
was thinking of filing a missing person's report.

A couple of days later, I got a call from one of the pastors and was asked to come in and talk. I was told that one of the parishioners had come into the church office (she overheard me talking on Sunday to the pastor—someone I didn't really know well) with a report about Hans and me.

This person took it upon herself to do a background check and brought in a list of public records. We had attended the church for over four years at this point, and everyone we knew well at the church was very much aware that Hans had a drinking problem. There were many people at the church who we knew were battling addictions themselves. The church's motto was, "We don't care where you have been; we care where you are going." This was important to Hans and me because we knew we had a past in which unfortunate things had happened to us.

At this meeting, I was asked to consider stepping down from my position on the church session as well as the pastoral search committee—first to take care of the girls and second because it would be an embarrassment to the church if the potential new pastor found out about our family's history. I was devastated. I certainly didn't want to be an embarrassment, but it was hurtful to be treated this way after four years of being very involved in our church's activities and programs. Later, I'd learn that that decision had not been discussed with the other session members. There were only a few who knew why I'd stepped down. The girls and I continued to attend the church because many of the people who knew our situation still reached out to us, prayed for us, and loved us. I tried to rise above the hurt and humiliation.

The following weekend, which was the first weekend in November, Hannah attended a Christian youth weekend retreat, which I knew Hans was very excited for her to attend. I was sure he would be coming back to support her. Hannah went to the retreat, and I thought if she needed to be anywhere, this was the best place for her—surrounded by people who would be better equipped to handle the situation if we got bad news.

Cross at Camp Lawrence

Sunday morning of that weekend, I received a call from a nurse at a hospital in Clarksville, Indiana, which was six hours south.

"We have Hans here in the emergency room," she said. "And he is reluctant to talk to you. Would you like to talk to him?"

I didn't want to but told her I would.

"Hello," I said.

"Hi," he replied, and there was a pause.

"I am truly sorry," he softly said.

I was thankful he was alive but furious at his selfishness. I did tell him to leave—but with the hope he would get the help he needed. Was this his rock bottom? The conversation was very short, maybe three minutes. I now knew he was alive. Yes, it was an answer to prayer, but where would we go from here?

I would find out that Hans had walked from Highway 65, picked up some alcohol, and checked himself into a hotel where, again, he was paying night by night to stay there. On the ninth day, the front desk received a call from someone staying at the hotel, saying there was a man in one of their rooms who needed help. They called paramedics, who found him in the hotel room passed out with several empty bottles of alcohol. Hans had been living off alcohol and nothing else for about a week and a half.

After I got off the call with Hans, I immediately texted a friend of mine that was at the youth camp with Hannah and asked her to relay the message that her dad was alive and in a hospital. Everyone had been praying, and God sure heard our prayers. I told Delaney, and she was so relieved. I went over to camp later that afternoon to talk with Hannah. We all definitely felt God's presence.

Hans had no car because it had been towed to a garage. He wanted to come home, but I told him no, I was not coming to get him. I was not driving twelve hours round trip. I had no desire to see him or where he was at. He called his friend, who also said *no*. Hans needed help. I thought the least I could do was to call around halfway houses in the Porter–LaPorte County area and even Porter Starke. I wasn't sure if I even wanted him around us or how he would get back. We all needed to get well, and it wasn't going to happen if he came home.

I talked with the hospital social worker and explained to her that it would not be in our family's best interest if he came back to the area. I asked her what his official diagnosis was.

"Alcohol-induced depression," she said.

That certainly made sense as the more he drank, the darker his mood became. I had no idea how to proceed or what would become of us.

> *God already knows the plans he has for us! Let go and let God.*

* * *

Hans

There is nothing so cruel in this world as the desolation of having nothing to hope for.
    —*Haruki Murakami*

Fall sunrises in Southern Indiana are spectacular. The trees are in brilliant colors, and there is a mist hanging over the ground like a shroud and a crispness to the air.

My perspective of the sunrise on October 30, 2014, was much different. I woke up cold, stiff, and not aware of my surroundings. As I groggily sat up and looked around, I realized that I was lying on the ground in a ditch by the side of a highway. The last thing I remembered from the day before was driving south on I-65 by Lafayette after stopping for food and vodka. I could not recall a single thing that had happened in the last twelve hours. As I sat up bleary-eyed, I saw a road sign about a hundred yards ahead of me, telling me that the next exit off I-65 was for Jeffersonville, Indiana—about 175 miles from Lafayette. I had no recollection even of driving through Indianapolis. My god.

I assessed my situation. I had no car or keys, but I know that I drove there. I had money in my pocket but no wallet and no phone to contact anyone. My first concern was not about my car or letting anyone know where I was but where I could find more vodka. The exit was not far ahead, so I started walking. After a few miles, I found a liquor store, but my problem was deciding how much to buy since I had to carry it all and did not have a place to sleep. I thought I would get enough for about two days, so I bought two half gallons and had them double-bagged so no one could tell what I was carrying, and I started off to find a hotel. An hour's walk brought me to a hotel that would take cash without an ID, as I had no wallet, and also give me a weekly rate. The bonus was that they had a continental breakfast, so I could spend all my money on alcohol.

Three days later, I gave up on going to the front desk for Danishes because I had no hunger for food and walking any distance at all was almost impossible. I found a local cabdriver who took me to the liquor store twice, and the third time, I had him come to the room and gave him money to buy more alcohol because I could barely stand. He was concerned about me and said that this was the last time he would do it, so I gave him even more money for a last run so I wouldn't run out.

Six more half gallons should just about be enough, I thought.

I was literally doing nothing except drinking and staring at the TV. My mind was numb, and I had no thoughts of the future other than I did not think that I was going to leave that room alive. About a week later, I was wasting some of the alcohol because I would drink it and immediately throw up, so I had to wait awhile until I could keep it down. I kept a glass by me so that when I vomited, I could try to get it in the glass and save it until I could keep it down. I was poisoning myself and praying that my body would just shut down and let me die. I did not even have the courage to end it suddenly but only excruciatingly slowly, one drink at a time. But God had other plans for me.

As I was lying on the bed, in and out of consciousness, I heard a pounding on the door and shouting. I tried to stand, but I fell and could not get up. After a few minutes, the door opened, and paramedics rushed in. When I mumbled about what was happening, they said that the front desk had gotten a call from the room, saying that someone needed help. It could not have been me. Moving was difficult, and talking on the phone was impossible. I do not know positively how that happened.

I know the facts, but there is not a logical explanation. There is, however, a spiritual explanation, which I choose to believe. My higher power intervened to keep me alive for another purpose that I did not understand yet. I had spent ten days at that hotel and lost over twenty pounds. As I was rushed to the hospital, I spent three days in detox while eating through an IV. I was considered a John Doe because I did not have any ID, and I was not talking to anyone because I was still trying to process what was happening and what I was going to do. The fourth morning I woke up, there was an Indiana state trooper standing at the foot of my bed. I thought my life was over. In reality, my life was just beginning.

This day I call the heavens and the earth as
witnesses against you that I have set before you life and
death, blessings and curses. Now choose life, so that you
and your children may live.
—*Deuteronomy 30:19*

That quote from Deuteronomy precisely describes what happened to me while lying on the bed in that hotel room. I had a choice, and with God's help, I made the right one, and I am alive.

The state trooper stood at the foot of the bed and then asked me my name. Even though I did not answer any questions from the hospital staff, including who I was, I felt compelled to answer the trooper. He then told me that my car was towed and impounded. Apparently, during a lane restriction at about 9:00 p.m., I had run over a few traffic barrels, stopped the car, and taken off. They brought out a K-9 to track me but couldn't find me. The car did not have any damage, but the keys were in it. I don't know how far I walked before I lay down in the ditch, but it was obviously far enough so the dog could not track me. He said they found an empty vodka bottle in the car, so he was pretty sure that I was drinking while I was driving.

Then came the first step on my real road to recovery. He said that since it happened a few days ago, there was nothing he could do. The only reason he was there was to make sure that I was okay and give me his card to call him if I needed anything—one of the first times I really understood and appreciated God's mercy. I asked him if he could get some clothes and my glasses out of the car. It had been two weeks since I had been able to see clearly, and I am extremely nearsighted. He also wanted to know if he could call anyone to let them know that I was okay.

This was an act of mercy that was another small step toward sobriety. Mercy is when we do not receive the bad things we deserve. In my mind, I was not deserving of anything positive at that time, yet the trooper only expressed concern, compassion, and a desire to help someone who could not help himself.

The nurse called Lisa and explained the situation and that I was physically okay. Lisa told my youngest daughter, and that morning, while my oldest daughter was at Awakening—which was the teen version of the church retreat called the Great

Banquet that I attended—a team member woke up Hannah and told her where her dad was and what happened. I did not know this until the next day, when I summoned up enough courage to call Lisa and talk to her. She was understandably extremely upset, but I could also tell that she was relieved that I did not end up in a morgue. I had left for almost two weeks without a word and abandoned her and my two daughters. There was no thought for her or the girls, and I was still having a hard time processing things in the shape that I was in.

After three days in the hospital, I was transferred to another rehab facility for observation and also to determine what to do with me. Because of my situation, I needed to be transported by ambulance while handcuffed to a gurney. The facility was more of a mental health facility, so I saw a lot of patients acting and talking very bizarrely, but I suddenly realized that this was probably how people saw me when I was drinking. Just as I did not want to be judged for my behavior, I was sure that they did not either.

I went to AA meetings two or three times a day and met with a counselor to decide on my next step. I was still very fragile emotionally, and the decision came down to a homeless shelter in Louisville or a halfway house in Jeffersonville. The halfway house was usually full, so I thought that I would end up homeless on the streets of Louisville. When the counselor called the halfway house, Jerry's Place, they had just had a discharge that morning, and if I could be there by that afternoon, I could have a bed. I am positive that if I was left to my own devices, the homeless shelter would have resulted in my death. That afternoon I was sent to Jerry's Place in a cab with no idea of what to expect.

Hans in Jeffersonville

Lisa

God will send the storm to show you he is the shelter.

Hans was released from the hospital to a halfway house called Jerry's Place in Jeffersonville, Indiana. I truly did not want Hans to come back until he got his act together. Even then, I was not sure I wanted to continue on this journey with him. I had had enough.

Jerry helped Hans get a job that he could walk to and from. Jerry's Place had strict rules. I was glad Hans was safe and working. I knew he could not go far because he did not have a vehicle. I sent him his phone, wallet, and a few other personal items. Because his work check was deposited into our joint account, I would send him $100 a week, $90 for room and board then the other $10 for personal items.

Hans wanted to take care of his family, even down in Southern Indiana. He was going to work, a daily AA meeting, and church, and he was focusing on his sobriety. I had a lot of resentment toward Hans for being so selfish and all about himself. There was no way I could have just checked out from parenting or working even though I'd wanted to many times. I too needed a break from all the emotional drama I had been through.

Every day Hans would call the girls and me. He would call in the morning before the girls went to school and then again in the evening. We kept the lines of communication open. I was happy Hans was making progress and getting better, but I was not sure, after all we had been through, if I could ever trust him again. Hans was not the guy I married, and I didn't sign up for this kind of life. I needed to keep all my options open.

I decided that I was going to see an attorney, not so much for a divorce as for legal separation. I wanted to clear myself from anything negative Hans might have done or might do. When Hans left and headed south, I was totally burnt out from life and our relationship. I was not sure which direction things were going to go. All I knew was, they could not keep going in the direction they were going.

I contacted my friend who'd used a local attorney for her divorce. I met with her lawyer and shared with him that I thought I wanted a legal separation. I did not want to be responsible for Hans's irresponsible choices. He asked why not a divorce, and I said because I wasn't sure if I wanted something so permanent. He told me that a legal separation was pretty much the same as a divorce. We continued to talk, and he asked me what assets we had. We only had a car. Then he asked me what else we had, and I said we'd filed a chapter 13, and we were in the middle of it.

He asked, "How much longer do you have in the bankruptcy?"

"Four years," I said.

The attorney looked at me and said, "Well, by law, you need to finish the bankruptcy before a divorce is granted. A bankruptcy surpasses a divorce. You will be considered married until the bankruptcy is discharged."

Wow! Wonderful! I thought. *How am I going to deal with this for another four years?*

The girls and I continued to live with our friends. I took the girls to school every day and picked them up. We continued to go to church and stay involved. The church was very good to the girls and me.

I wanted the girls to get some counseling after Hans headed south. I was concerned about their emotional well-being. I was referred to a counselor in Valparaiso.

One day, in the car with Delaney, I said, "I know things have been hard lately with Dad, and I think you need to talk to someone."

She said, "I am not going to talk to anyone. I already know what is going on. My dad has an alcohol disease. It is not my fault, and he is getting help."

Well, that pretty much summed it up.

When I told Hannah I was going to have her talk to someone, she just came straight out and said, "No, I am not going."

I heard the girls, but my decision stood. The church we attended agreed to pay for their counseling sessions. I picked them up from school without telling them and drove them to the appointment. When we arrived, they refused to get out of the car. I told them the appointment was made. We needed to at least give it a try, and after pleading with them, they went into the appointment. The counselor was very nice, and the girls liked him. The girls continued with their counseling sessions, and it seemed to help.

Hannah's 9th grade Madrigal Dinner

Christmas 2014, Minnesota

Papa always teaching the girls new things

Cross at Lisa's mom's cemetery

Every so often your loved ones will open the door and visit our dreams . . . Thanks, Mom, for always watching over us.

Lisa's 50th birthday

Hans sends Lisa flowers for her fiftieth

* * *

Hans

The cab pulled up to an old one-story house with some outbuildings across from a cemetery. I walked into the house and heard a gruff voice shout out, "I'll be right there."

Jerry turned out to be an older recovering alcoholic whose only desire in life was to help addicts recover. He explained the rules to me: ninety dollars per week in rent, share a room with another addict, daily meetings at the house, keep your room clean, and above all, *no* alcohol or drugs. It didn't sound all that good, but I really had no choice. My money was running out, so I called my friend—whose wife gave me my *Life Recovery Bible* and who said that he would help with rent for a month.

I was hoping to go home in a week or so, but he convinced me that it would do no one any good to have me return that soon. This same friend has been in my life through all the stages— beginning in our twenties, with us playing air guitar at 3:00 a.m. in the middle of Duval Street outside Sloppy Joe's in Key West; then him helping me out when I was at Jerry's; to having dinner recently, when he strongly encouraged me to read Deuteronomy, where I found the quote that started this chapter.

He promised to send the rent money to Jerry because I know that he did not want to send me cash. Lisa then sent $100 a week to pay for room and board as well as $10 a week for miscellaneous items.

After a few days of this, I walked by a liquor store and turned in and bought another half gallon, telling myself lies from the moment I walked in the door until I got back to Jerry's. At the meeting that night, I stumbled in and was walked back out immediately by Jerry and another resident. This time I was sent to the local hospital, which had a detox area and where I spent another three days.

More meetings, more counseling. I was just starting to realize that alcohol was *not* my problem. *I* was my problem. I did things to numb myself and escape from my reality. What I really needed to do was change my reality. When you come to the depths of an addiction, it is called hitting rock bottom.

Rock bottom is different for everyone, from losing a job, divorce, all the way to death. When you do hit rock bottom, you either give up fully or bounce back. It is the point where there is no way to rationalize drinking again. At that point, I gave up fully on myself but not on life. Recovery is not easy, but when the pain of staying the same is worse than the pain of change, it is when change can truly happen. I literally had nothing to fall back on. I was mentally and physically completely empty.

Jerry's Place

Jerry allowed me to come back on the terms that if I violated the rules again, he would not take me to the hospital; he would call the police. That night I sobbed in my room until I cried myself to sleep. I've always heard the saying that grown men don't cry. I do not know if that is true, but I do know that growing men do.

I spent my days walking, going to the library, and thinking. Step 1 of AA is that you admit that you are powerless over alcohol and your life had become unmanageable. When I looked at it objectively, I realized where I was and why—powerless and unmanageable. I always thought that admitting it meant that I was weak. It is completely the opposite. Criss Jami said, "When you show weakness, you make yourself vulnerable, and when you make yourself vulnerable, it shows your strength." When I confronted it, I could start to deal with it. How do I get that control and manage my life?

At AA meetings, I heard a lot of suggestions, and some came from alcoholics with decades of sobriety. When I came to the realization that I was the problem and alcohol was my medication, I knew that I had to fix myself first. I could not stop drinking without help.

The environment at Jerry's allowed me to practice sobriety in alcohol-free surroundings with daily meetings as reinforcement. Jerry had connections with a factory owner who occasionally hired residents of the halfway house. I walked the two miles to and from the factory every day, which gave me time to think. I befriended someone at the factory who also had an alcohol addiction, but he was overcoming his by walking to and from the plant every day from prison on work release. He had thirty minutes to get to work and thirty minutes to get back, or they would send an officer to look for him. He had multiple DUIs and killed someone with his last one, and he had six years left on his prison sentence. He agonized every day about what he had done.

I know that his daily walks to work were far from therapeutic for him like mine were to me. He was paid the same as everyone else but only got to keep twenty-five cents per hour for himself, with the rest going to the prison. But he also felt blessed to be able to have the diversion of work as he did not feel that he deserved it. He suffered every day because he was a good soul and he was in prison—not the jail cell or a menial job but a prison in his mind of never being able to forgive himself for taking a life. That was where he suffered the most.

I walked by an empty field on the way to work that had a few abandoned railroad boxcars in it, and I was always puzzled by the fact that there were footprints in the snow leading to and from them. I asked someone at work about them, and they told me that a few people lived in the boxcars in the winters to try to stay warm. I was curious about it and watched the field after work for a while. I saw some people approach the boxcars and was stunned when I saw some adults and four younger children get in the boxcars. It did not even cross my mind that children would have to live in those conditions. A few days later, I stopped seeing the tracks. I knew there was one of two outcomes, but I did not think about it much because I couldn't bear to think about the negative one.

I went to meetings every day and sometimes twice on weekends. One hundred ninety meetings in one hundred eighty days, and church every Sunday, was my final tally. I listened and learned and finally started to understand some things about my addiction. It was at church that I truly came to believe that a power greater than myself could restore me to sanity, which was step 2. Jesus only came into my life when our daughters were born and we wanted to expose them to the church. I went, but it was more of a casual acquaintance with Jesus than true faith. I experienced true faith from the congregation at that church and came to know the power of God. I read spiritual books, and with the continuing understanding of Jesus, he became more and more a part of my life.

A close friend, Ron, gave Lisa a book for Christmas that year, and she thought I might like it. So she sent me *The Case for Christ* by Lee Strobel. Reading it completely changed how I saw religion. It paired faith with fact to where they supported each other, and all of a sudden, things made so much sense from a spiritual standpoint.

Faith is belief without proof, and fact is something proven to be true, but *The Case for Christ* tied faith and fact together and connected the gap between needing proof and not needing it. I read it three times during my stay at Jerry's, and each time, I found something new. I was always a person who had a much easier time believing in things if I could see, hear, or touch them. True faith involved none of those things. Then my perspective changed to where I could not see Jesus, but I saw people acting with grace, mercy, and humility. I could not hear Jesus, but I heard people talk about how their lives were transformed by Jesus. I could not touch Jesus, but Jesus reached out to touch me spiritually.

The residents of Jerry's Place had a small Christmas party, and I saw the guys' families together for the first time. It showed me a little of the humanity that this disease could steal from you—people who loved each other and were saddened and confused at the situation they were in, hoping that things would get better soon.

This was the first time that I had seen firsthand what utter chaos we alcoholics cause in other people's lives. The closer those people are to us, the more they are traumatized. Unfortunately, it was not like that for some of the residents. Jail was the only other option the legal system gave some of them—six months at Jerry's or six months in jail. Very few of those men made the six months at Jerry's. They broke the rules, relapsed, or in a couple of extreme cases, died.

The men who took recovery seriously did well in the program. I had gotten into a routine of work, meetings, dinner, books, and sleep, and I was starting to feel healthy. My wants were few, but my needs were great. I needed stability, meetings, low stress, and a positive environment, and Jerry's was where I was getting them. Some of the residents who were not interested in staying sober did not become a trigger to my relapse but to my recovery. I started to see alcoholism from the other side.

My job became eight hours of paid sobriety instead of the drudgery most other employees felt, and meetings became a place to share and listen to others. My spiritual reading in the evenings allowed me to process God. When I spoke to Lisa and my daughters, I noticed that we were all becoming emotionally healthier. The time apart was allowing everyone to heal without the pressure of my alcoholism there every day. We talked about what we were all doing and feeling and taking baby steps.

Fortunately, those baby steps were all going forward. Some of the other residents at Jerry's had huge life changes just in the time that I was there.

George F. took me to his Baptist church, and the parishioners were passionate, to say the least. Also having that type of passion led George to thrive at Jerry's and in recovery. He was someone whom I looked up to for his indomitable spirit.

Another resident who owned a local plumbing company at one time was married and had kids but lost it all through his alcoholism. He was asked to leave Jerry's when he was caught in bed with a bottle of vodka next to him. He was found in a local park about a week later, frozen to death. He did not have any services that we could attend.

I saw some of the residents every day for six months, and some of them were only there for a couple of days before relapsing. I always wondered why it ended up that way. I was fortunate that at the time, my life was simplified, and my mind was not cluttered with a myriad of things pulling at my sobriety.

*Sobriety is not the gates of heaven opening to let
me in; it is the gates of hell opening to let me out.*
—*AA saying*

I mentioned that I realized I was the problem. Instead of using alcohol to try to fix myself, I needed a different solution. The negative thoughts about myself and life in general kept me mired in the quicksand that was alcoholism. Occasionally, people will say that they had an "aha" moment, or something hit them like a bolt of lightning.

I was at an AA meeting when I heard something that gave me instant clarity. Someone said that they were looking at sobriety completely wrong. They always thought that sobriety would open the gates of heaven to let them in, but then after a few months, they would always relapse. They said that they needed to change their perspective and look at it like sobriety was actually the gates of hell opening and letting them out. I always expected that sobriety was a fix for everything in my life. In reality, sobriety only allows you to live a life without the weight and restrictions of addiction. It freed me to make decisions that would benefit me instead of harming me. My thoughts and actions started to become based on clear thinking, and I started to become more of the person I was before my addiction—a good, caring person who also had a lot of faults, just like everyone else.

My faith started to become even more important to me, and I took step 3 of AA. I turned my will and my life over to the care of God as I understood him. In addition to Jerry's, I went to meetings at a local church on weekends, and the people attending were people with sobriety from twenty-four hours up to forty years. They were doctors, lawyers, fast-food workers, unemployed, factory workers, politicians, business owners—basically showing that every walk of life could be affected by alcoholism. This was where I met my sponsor, someone who helped guide me through the twelve-step program.

I had gotten through the first three steps by myself, and now I started to work on step 4, taking a searching and fearless inventory of my life. I knew that it was not going to be pretty. It took me a few weeks of thinking and writing to get everything onto only forty-three pages. Wow.

Next was step 5—admitting to God, ourselves, and another human being the exact nature of our wrongs. Admitting to God and myself my wrongs was not easy, but it was nothing compared to admitting it to another human being. My sponsor and I sat down for three sessions of about two hours each, and I was exhausted after each session. The emotional energy I expended during these sessions was almost overwhelming.

About this time, another situation arose back in Valparaiso that Lisa had to deal with and strained my sobriety. The church that we attended and where Lisa was on a committee decided to take action against our family based on information that they had. The fact that we had been regular attendees and all of a sudden I was not there anymore started a number of rumors. Someone at the church took it upon themselves to do a criminal background check on me and found my OWI and a previous minor charge.

At this point, the interim pastor told Lisa that our family situation was an embarrassment to the church, and she was asked to step down from the committee. Lisa and the girls had to deal with this on a weekly basis, every Sunday. It was made a little easier by the fact that there were still good people who stood by Lisa and the girls. The church also made sure that Lisa and the girls had availability for counseling. The reason the church had an interim pastor was that the former pastor needed to retire due to health reasons. He and I were close, and he was a good friend and counselor.

Apparently, after retirement, pastors are not supposed to have contact with former parishioners. When one church member found out that we were still talking regularly, they notified the local presbytery to report him. I could not fathom how getting help for my addiction could be construed as wrong.

In the past, these things would have instantly led me to the bottle and definitely away from God. In my current state of mind, I knew that these things were done by humans and had nothing to do with God. It was crucial to move past this, and my main concern was for Lisa and the girls and how they would react to it. They found that a few isolated people would not challenge their faith. During this time, other church members made sure that Lisa and my daughters could get counseling and were okay emotionally. Rarely is any organization or group of people all bad or all good. There are still many of the church members who are dear friends to us.

There are only three outcomes for alcoholics. They are sobriety, jail, or death. In the time that I was at Jerry's, I witnessed all three. Recovery does not take any days off. It needs to be monitored daily. My focus was shifting to positive things. Your perspective on almost all things in life will shape your attitude. I started to look at what I did have instead of what I didn't. Gratitude was allowing me to be appreciative of my health, family, and future. Instead of complaining about how little money I made, I thought of how much it was helping Lisa and the girls get by. Instead of complaining about how long the walk was to work and meetings, I thought about how lucky I was to have the time to process my life without interruption. Instead of thinking how hard it was going to be to go back to Chesterton, I thought about how blessed I was to have a family who loved me.

Hans Returns from Southern Indiana

Lisa

May you have the courage to break the patterns in your life that are no longer serving you!

I t was a Thursday in March of 2015 when Hans came back to Valparaiso for the first time after heading south. I met him at the bus station in Merrillville. The girls didn't know he was coming home for a visit. He had returned to take care of some legal issues. It was one of the first times he'd decided to own up to his responsibilities.

I was a little apprehensive to see him. We went to a restaurant to talk before heading back to Valparaiso. Hans looked good, and I could definitely tell he was at peace. Hans stayed with his cousin who lived in Kouts, Indiana. I was very proud of Hans for owning up and dealing with the legal stuff he had run away from. We knew it wasn't the end of the chaos but also knew it was the beginning of the healing process for our family. God was in control, and we needed to follow his lead. It was the first time I felt in my heart that Hans really got the importance of sobriety and recovery and acknowledged the miracle of God giving him another chance at life. He also had the girls and me here to support him as long as he did the work.

Hans and I went to pick the girls up from school that Friday afternoon. We first went to get Hannah, and the look on her face was priceless. Then we went to pick up Delaney, and she too was excited to see him. We had dinner together as a family and did some catching up. The next day we took a wonderful family trip to Chicago. We loved going to Chicago as a family. Taking the train, shopping, and pizza at Gino's East all made for a perfect day. We had such a good time. It was so nice to be together as a family again, laughing and making memories.

Chicago, March 2015, Hans home for a visit

After Hans finished dealing with his legal issues, I dropped him off at the bus station to head back to Jeffersonville.

Hans and I started talking about him coming back to Northwest Indiana. What would it look like? Was he ready? Were the girls and I ready? Would we live together or stay separated? Where would he get a job? There were so many unanswered questions and many things to take into consideration.

We had created our new normal, and the healing felt good. I definitely did not want to rush him or myself. I wasn't totally at peace with everything, but I knew I loved Hans, and he was a great husband and dad when he was sober. I also knew God would take care of whatever was to come our way because we now started to have faith in God's journey for us.

You could say that the past five years leading up to Hans leaving to go south were like this verse in 1 Kings 17:7, "the brook ran dry," and the only thing that we had left was our faith in God. You don't know God is all you need until God is all you have. Everything dried up in our life—money, housing, energy. We were in a hopeless place, and we needed a miracle.

Hans and I reached out to some friends to see if anyone might be willing to rent Hans a room and if anyone knew of a pet-friendly place the girls and I could rent. Immediately Hans heard from a friend of ours from the Lutheran church we attended. We knew them but hadn't really been in touch.

Our friends did not ask any questions. They were very gracious to Hans, and the wife wanted to make sure he felt at home. I felt a little resentful because Hans was taking baby steps reentering into our family. He was independent and could call his shots. By "shots," I mean, when he wanted alone time, when he wanted to see the girls, and when he wanted to see me. He didn't have to be responsible for the girls all the time or anything else he didn't want to do. I still took care of all the finances and everything with our daughters. Things were still rocky between us. I never realized what a routine-dependent person Hans was until we went through this journey. I was skeptical because we had been down this road before. I told myself we needed to trust the journey, whatever it looked like. I was exhausted yet found the strength to keep moving forward.

Not only did Hans need a place to live, but he also needed a job. What was he going to do? I suggested he reach out to a company owned by a family we knew that was similar to the company he'd worked for in Southern Indiana. When he called and spoke to one of the brothers, he said, "We don't have a job currently, but let me see what I can come up with."

A couple of days later, Hans got a call and was told, "We have a position for you." A truly answered prayer. Thank you, Jesus.

After six months of Hans being cut off from everything, he came back to Porter County in April 2015 from Southern Indiana, ready to start his new life. Miracles do happen . . .

He had a new job, had been sober for six months, and was feeling awesome. Although he was happy and regaining his life, which I had prayed for, I still felt a huge resentment toward him and all he put us through. I had a hard time letting go of all the disappointments, and I seemed to be constantly on edge, waiting for the next unexpected thing to happen. Hans had six months on his own to gain control of his sobriety and had no other responsibilities but himself. In the meantime, I was still having to work, take care of the girls, pay the bills, take care of the dog, take care of myself, and so much more. I felt I needed a recovery period for myself as well.

Sometimes I just looked up, smiled, and said, "I know that was you, God! Thanks for being by my side!"

My friends would say, "You need to take care of yourself, Lisa . . . for the girls."

What the heck? How could I take care of myself when I was on autopilot taking care of everything else? I was so thankful for my village mommas, who stepped in to take care of the girls, take me out to lunch, called me daily to check in, and prayed for us. It was also important to me that I tried to provide a stable, consistent, and nurturing environment for my daughters. I wanted to surround them with as much normalcy as I could. It was important to keep regular traditions and family rituals, like Christmas, holiday celebrations, and birthdays. We always found a way to visit family in Minnesota and keep the girls involved in their activities. They didn't deserve to live in a home of chaos.

After Hans had lived with our friends for a couple of months, we still weren't sure if we wanted to live together. Not until we knew in our hearts that we could move beyond where we were at. There was a lot of broken trust and chaos to overcome. Our lives were turned upside down.

I eventually found a two-bedroom duplex to rent in Valparaiso for the girls and me. Was it a nice place? Well, it was clean, inexpensive, livable, would take Polly, and wasn't in the basement of someone's house. With a little TLC, I knew we could make it our own. I knew it was just a stepping-stone to get us back on our feet. The girls always seemed to go with the flow as long as we were together. It was also very important for me to keep the girls attending the same school district with their friends.

Duneland schools were very good about out-of-district students attending. It was an adjustment for all of us to be together again in Valparaiso.

One day, Hannah and I were driving in the car, and she said to me, "Mom, God knew what he was doing when Dad got sick."

"What do you mean?" I said.

"We wouldn't know all the wonderful people that are our friends today if Dad wouldn't have gotten sick."

"Wow, you are so right," I said.

That was the logic from a ninth grader who had always been wiser than her years.

If you want the struggle to end . . . be grateful!

Our family life was going to look different, with a new normal. I had to let go of what I thought my life was going to be and come to terms with what was. Over the years, I always needed to know what was going on. I got very anxious if I wasn't prepared or in the know. I needed my finger on everything. I wanted to have control over my life as well as Hans's and the girl's lives. I controlled the finances, where we went on vacation, where we moved, what we bought, what Hans wore, where he worked, and what the girls did. The more chaotic things became, the more codependent I was.

I kept adding to my plate . . . Every day no one would leave the house without their clothes ironed. I made the girls' lunches every day for school, drove the girls to school every day, and picked them up. I was a helicopter wife and mother. You could say it got to the point I was smothering everyone, trying to keep them close. I became mentally distraught. I had to learn that I had little to no control. I needed to let go and believe God would handle things in our lives. He was the one who knew the plans he had for us and what the outcome would be.

In June 2015, shortly after Hans returned from Southern Indiana, I was so happy when he went with a group of Christian guys on a weekend trip to Manistee, Michigan. I prayed that God would provide Hans with good Christian friends and followers of Jesus whom he could relate to as well as develop a relationship with. Hans is an introvert, and I am very much an extrovert. Hans always seemed content being by himself, and this made me very uncomfortable. I always believed you need to surround yourself with a community of people who would be there for you and help you grow as a person.

In August, Hans gradually started spending more time at the duplex with the girls and me. The duplex was three blocks from Hans's work. We were starting over, catching up on our bills.

In 2014, when Hannah started high school, she made it into the Show Choir. I was so excited for her. Singing and dancing were her outlets. The fees were a little steep for us as we were just getting back on our feet.

I had remembered going to an outside fair once with Hans and seeing a booth selling gourmet seasonings. I reached out to the wholesale company. I thought if we could buy some dips, we could sell them to help raise money for Hannah's show choir fees. My entrepreneurial mind kicked in. The company had a minimum of one hundred dips you needed to purchase at $1 each. Somehow, I found the money to do just that. We ended up selling some dips to family and friends to help offset the cost of the show choir. After we had moved into the duplex in Valparaiso and I was unpacking some boxes, I ran across the dips again. We must have had fifty packets left. What were we going to do with all these extras?

One weekend Hans and I drove by a farmers' market in New Buffalo, Michigan, and I called the owner to ask her how much it was to rent a space. She said $30 and told us we could come on a Saturday to see how it would work out. So we found a tent, a table, and a couple of chairs. We set up a booth with the intention of selling our inventory. That first Saturday, we practically sold out of almost all the seasonings we had. We thought, *Wow, this is fun and profitable.* We took some of our profits and ordered more seasonings. We had absolutely no intention of starting a small business, but the opportunity presented itself. We had a little extra money. It was easy. The girls could help us. All the market items fit into our car, and it was good to have a new and positive environment to be a part of. This was how Dippity Dips was started.

Summer after Hans came back

*We must meet people where they are at . . . We
can't assume we know what's best for them.*

It seemed as we continued to take one day at a time and do
the next right thing, our life started to fall into place. I had no idea
how God was going to use us, but every day we needed to show
up and meet that day's opportunities. Life started to settle into a
new norm.

During our time in Valparaiso, we could have focused on all
the things we did not have: the big house, a second car, certainty
and assurances, etc. We could have fixated on all the negativity
and on feeling hopeless, or we could focus on trusting we were
exactly where we were supposed to be. I won't say it was easy to
change or accept this path, but as Hans reminded me regularly,
"It is easy to stay doing what you are doing. Change is hard but
worth it."

My healing came from educating myself about addiction and
codependency. I had to look within to see how I was a contributor
to our family issues. I was blinded by my own imperfections
and unhealthy patterns. I also found healing in helping others. I
intentionally made it a point to give back to others as others had
unselfishly given to us. I had to remind myself that just because
our family had to walk through the darkness of addiction, this

was our journey to heal. If you have been given God's grace and mercy, it is easier to give grace to others. We may have not had a lot financially, but we had all we needed. We had food, shelter, clothing, our health, a community of friends that loved us, and our *faith*. We were abundantly rich by God's grace and mercy.

In November 2015, Hannah was asked to give a talk at the Christian teen retreat about her walk with Jesus. Hannah was fifteen and very mature for her age. I look back to when I was her age and remember never wanting anyone to know what was going on in our family. No one wanted to admit that their family had issues. A part of the healing process for our family was being able to share our story with others and to give hope to those going through similar things.

I was very proud of Hannah when she stood up in front of a room full of teen girls and many adults and said, "Hi, my name is Hannah Scheller. I am fifteen years old, a sophomore in high school, and my dad is an alcoholic."

The first step to any recovery is admitting there is a problem and owning it.

Family...Grateful, Thankful and Blessed

Very proud of our Hannah for giving a very powerful message today with such grace, confidence and lovingness! Being God's light to shine in others. God definitely has amazing plans for you! I am truly blessed to be your Momma!!!! Love you!!!

God always showed up, and we never knew whom he would put in our path. I met another good friend while working with Junior Achievement. My friend was a counselor at one of the schools I worked with. We had a meeting one day, and as I was leaving, she asked me how I knew some mutual friends. I told her that it was through a Christian community we belonged to. She asked me to sit down with her, and she told me about some life challenges she was going through. I shared with her how this Christian community changed our lives. I told her that Hans and I would be more than willing to sponsor both her and her husband at the upcoming retreat. My friend went home to talk to her husband, and the next thing I knew, they both wanted to go.

Both the men's and women's retreats were on different weekends. The men's weekend was first. I had only known my friend and never met her husband before. We went to dinner with some mutual friends so that we could all get to know each other. Both our friends went to their retreats and had a wonderful time. Both my friend and her husband quickly became good friends of ours.

The first two years after Hans returned from Southern Indiana, life had its obstacles; it was not perfect. But no matter what . . . God was working in our family's life. God placed people in our lives we would have never met otherwise. He opened doors that we never could have imagined, and with prayer and commitment, things started to move in a more positive direction with many blessings. Because of God's grace, our family has experienced a new life. God's grace isn't what he has already done for us but the power he gives us to move forward. Grace fuels our faith.

Girls at the duplex in Valparaiso

Christmas after Hans returned

* * *

Hans

After a few months of sobriety, I carefully started to think about what my next steps would be. I was not going to stay at Jerry's long term. I knew that I had some legal issues to deal with in LaPorte County. The money I had taken needed to be accounted for, and the relationships I had destroyed had to be repaired. I never wavered in wanting to face these things as soon as I could.

I found out that there was a warrant for my arrest in LaPorte County, so I contacted an attorney, who asked how I wanted to deal with this. I told him that I could take a couple of days off work and come up there and deal with it. I took a bus from Louisville and met Lisa in Merrillville, where we had some awkward moments. Anything that I said was going to be too much and also not enough. We did not talk about the future very much, only tried to deal with the immediate issue. She knew how much I loved her, and I knew how much she loved me.

We went to Chicago on a family outing and had a great time even though it was a little uneasy. When I went to the courthouse to turn myself in and bond out until my court date, I found out there was also a warrant in Porter County for a probation violation. LaPorte County was going to hold me until they could move me to Porter County to deal with those charges. I spent two days waiting for the transfer.

Chicago spring break 2015, Hans home for a visit

At first I stayed totally to myself, but after listening to the other inmates, I realized that alcohol and drugs or the actions from using them were the reasons that almost all of them were there. As we talked, some of them told me that they desperately wanted to get sober or clean and that some others had resigned themselves to the fact that they would be dealing with substance abuse and the legal system for the rest of their lives. For many of them, it was the only life that they had ever known. They grew up with drugs and/or alcohol constantly around them and felt they had no choice except to go back to that lifestyle when they were paroled.

I was moved to Porter County, where my attorney managed to get me released almost immediately. He was a friend from my time working at the Boys & Girls club and thought enough of me that he fronted the bond money for me so that I could get back to Jeffersonville before I lost my job there. I said goodbye to Lisa but did not discuss the future, only that I would be back in a month for court. I arrived back in Jeffersonville at about 1:00 a.m. and was ready to go back to work the next day.

I had been talking to my daughters on almost a daily basis and did not try to hide what was going on. They had seen the addiction at its worst and seemed pretty resilient through it. They knew that I was safe and working on getting healthy. We discussed things that were happening in our lives and did focus on the future but only day-to-day. When they were younger, they saw me as a loving father with behavioral issues. They began to understand the correlation of the behavior with the action that caused it. I *always* tried to hide my drinking from everyone, but the girls knew what the cause of my erratic behavior was. I could hide the consumption but not the actions stemming from it. They were having to deal with adult problems with a child's mind, and it was hard to process. Their faith in God helped them realize that there was a reason for my alcoholism even if they could not understand it at the time. This was more motivation for me to be honest and up front.

One thing that all alcoholics do well is lie. We lie to cover things up, get out of consequences, acquire things, and make ourselves look good until it becomes as easy as breathing. A major hurdle was crossed when one day I realized that it was easier for me to tell the truth than to lie. It was a great weight off me when the consequences of telling the truth were not going to embarrass me or get me in trouble.

Through all this, I was seeing the mercy and grace that was bestowed on me. Mercy is when God does not punish us for the things that we deserve, and grace is when we are blessed but do not deserve it. I went back to Jerry's and started to take on more responsibility around the house. Keeping residents on track by counseling them on sobriety, work, rules of the house, and generally getting by in a positive way were some of the things I tried to help with. My employer asked me to consider a promotion. I could have taken it for the extra money, but I knew that I would probably be leaving soon, so I declined it and explained that I did not want to get trained and take the extra money from them if I was going to be leaving soon. They were very supportive and offered to help in any way to help me transition back to my old life. It was around this time that I had to face the reality of going back out on my own and making decisions based solely on my own abilities. Being in rehab, a halfway house, or even jail, to a certain extent, was somewhat isolating. Many positive decisions were made for you if you could carry them out.

This was when I did step 6 and, shortly after that, step 7. Step 6 is when you are entirely ready to have God remove your defects of character. I came to Jerry's completely broken and ready to be molded anew. I actually had *no* character left, whether positive or defective. Once I was ready, it was not exactly time to ask God to actually remove them, which was step 7. I prayed that when my character traits were instilled in me again, the defects would be left out.

> *Please give me acceptance and not judgment, give me humility and not arrogance, give me patience and not anxiety, give me hope and not fear, give me empathy and not apathy, give me tranquility and not anger, give me faith and not doubt, but mostly instill in me love and not hate.*

There were a lot of things that needed to happen before I could move back to Chesterton. I had to find employment, deal with the court issues, and find a place to live because Lisa and I had decided that we would not live together right away. These were some very large obstacles to be dealt with. Stress had always been a trigger for me, and I was feeling stressed about multiple things. This was when grace entered my life in full force. I put on a social media page that I was considering moving back to the area and for anyone to let me know if there was an inexpensive apartment or someone who needed a roommate.

Hans

Within a day, I had a response from a couple whom Lisa and I knew from a church we attended a number of years back. We were social friends but had mostly lost touch over the years. They told me that they had an extra bedroom that I could stay in for as long as I needed to. It was an amazingly generous gesture that still makes me emotional.

My attorney was working on my court case, and by paying a fine and full restitution, I would not need to go to jail but only be on probation. I did not have any fear of violating probation because I knew that if I had a major relapse, a probation violation would be the least of my worries.

For a job, I put out over a hundred résumés on job-search websites without a single response. If I was not employed, having court resolved and a place to stay meant nothing because I could not move without income. Lisa suggested that I call a company whose owners had taken over their family business. The new owners were members of the Boys & Girls Club that I worked at for eleven years, and I got to know the family there. I thought that it might be a good fit because the company I worked for in Jeffersonville was a plastic injection molding company. The company in Valparaiso was also a plastic injection molding company. When I spoke to the owners, they were looking for someone to oversee and supervise the production employees. They took a chance on me when no one else would. When I got my business degree about thirty years ago, I only had to take a couple of classes in order to get another degree—in supervision. I ended up getting the job in Valparaiso. A place to stay, no jail time, and a job all within two weeks. Albert Einstein said, "Coincidence is God's way of remaining anonymous."

Gratitude changes the pangs of memory into a tranquility.
—Dietrich Bonhoeffer

A cab took me away from Jerry's just like a cab brought me there. At 5:00 a.m., I was dropped off at the bus station in Louisville to catch the bus that would take me back to Northwest Indiana. Two large garbage bags were all the physical baggage I had, but I had plenty of mental baggage.

I had a place to stay but did not know if I would fit well with the family. I had a job but did not know if I could perform it well. I had my court issues under control, yet I did not know if it would haunt me in the future. Going home to a family who loved me and never gave up on me was my rock. You cannot start again, but you can start now with a new end. Sobriety will not restore you, but it will renew you. Stress and pressure were two of my largest triggers for relapse, and I wasn't sure exactly what was waiting for me back home.

When I arrived at my friends' home, they welcomed me with open arms and made me feel completely at ease. There was no pressure, only acceptance, and no timeline needed to live by.

Once there I started to work on step 8. I made a list of all persons I had harmed and became willing to make amends to them all. As I was working on step 8, I started step 9—to make direct amends to such people wherever possible, except when to do so would injure them or others. I still work on those two on a continual basis.

I was on probation and started to pay my court costs, so that aspect of life was good. When I started my job, it was exactly what I needed to succeed. The owners were supportive, proactive, and empowering without micromanaging. I could find something to relate to with everyone at work because I had been in almost everyone's shoes there—business owner, supervisor, machine operator, laborer, immigrant, and both struggling and successful. In my recovery, it was crucial to have an environment of stability without being smothered.

Lisa and I went to a wedding reception for a daughter of some friends, and we knew that there was going to be an open bar there and probably a lot of drinking. It was going to be a test for me to see how I handled it and reacted to the situations that would arise. After dinner, the bar opened again, and the first thing I had to deal with was a situation that happens at a lot of wedding receptions. It is when you have the one person who starts dancing alone *way* too early in the evening. It was almost an out-of-body experience seeing someone lose most of their inhibition, composure, and coordination minute by minute. It was really the first time I had seen someone drunk in quite a while. My thoughts could have gone a number of different ways, but mostly I felt sorry for the person—not pity but sympathy, because I had been there many times.

Lisa and I did not drink, and we socialized with people who didn't, so we had a very good time. As we were leaving the reception at about 1:00 a.m., my sobriety spoke up and told me that nobody should even get in a car that quite a few of these people were driving. Every single headlight I saw on the way home made me think about who was driving that car and what was the person doing. I had been behind those headlights many times in my past.

May 2015 after Hans returned from Southern Indiana

Hans with Hannah at her spring concert

The final adjustment was the most important one—my family. When I came back, my daughters were twelve and fourteen years old and had never seen me any different other than the alcoholic I was when I left. The only person they knew was alternately loving, caring, and supportive along with neglectful, self-absorbed, and drunk most of the time.

Just as stability was important to my recovery, they needed to have a stable environment to thrive. Lisa and I did not provide that for them. Physically, it was constantly moving, lack of money, cars being repossessed, bankruptcy, and my Jekyll and Hyde behavior. One thing that they always did have, though, was an abundance of love and a strong support group.

Our family and friends were there for the girls when I was not. We started out tentatively because neither side knew what to expect. I felt that they had every right to be resentful and unforgiving, and they did not know if this time it could actually be different. I had to prove myself every day, and they had to be willing to allow me back into their lives a little bit at a time. When I started to appreciate the little things more and focus on the positive, my behavior started to improve. Instead of dwelling on the argument I had with the girls, I thought of ways to avoid the argument. Sobriety was giving me a relationship with reality, and while that reality was not always where I wanted to be, it also gave me the ability to change it.

As much as addicts in recovery want things to move at a fast pace, patience is key. We need to enjoy the journey and appreciate the positive changes that are happening during recovery.

I was cognizant of the little things that were happening during the early days—such as waking up clearheaded, not wanting to pull into every liquor store that I saw, and being honest with myself and others. Lying was easy during active abuse because if I told the truth, I would get in trouble as most of the things that I was doing were not good. Lying to others also made me feel that they were also lying to me because that was just what people did to cover up for their actions. I never realized how crucial telling the truth was. I can now be myself without feeling ashamed or depressed.

I spent most of my life trying to become someone. I never knew that the whole time, I already was someone. I did not have to create myself. Addition was not the answer; subtraction was. All that I needed to do was remove the things that were not really *me*. A resistance to Jesus, always needing to impress people, arrogance, and knocking people down to build myself up are some of the things that are not truly who I am; and eliminating those things revealed to myself and others who Hans Scheller was meant to be.

A few months after I returned to Valparaiso, I was asked to go on a weekend church retreat in Michigan with about thirty other men. We had conversations about Jesus and where he was in our lives; we talked about personal issues and what was going well. I was still feeling new things in my sobriety, but that weekend gave me a lot of clarity.

There were many strong men in faith that weekend as well as many who were weak and struggling. It was a time of reflection and processing my life that resulted in me gaining the ability to see multiple sides of a situation. I slept on the ground and was bitten by mosquitos constantly. I also shared fellowship and heard inspirational things from good men.

The weekend culminated in a Sunday church service at the campground. Everyone was going to pack up after the service to head back home. The weather had been good all weekend, but that morning, it was cloudy with some ominous-looking clouds. As the service was about to end, it started to drizzle on us. After the last words by the pastor, a mad rush ensued to try to get things packed up quickly and stay dry. I stood in the light rain and truly thought about what was happening. Someone asked me why I wasn't getting ready to go, and I said, "After the great weather we've had, I think that the rain is God's way of baptizing the weekend, and I am going to enjoy it a little longer." Perspective had found its place in my soul. The quote "I wish you enough rain to appreciate the sunshine" came into my head.

As with most things in life, there are ups and downs, and no one is immune to them. Jesus turned water into wine, and I saw sobriety turn into food, shelter, and clothing. After a few months, Lisa and I decided to live together again.

We found a small two-bedroom duplex close to where I worked. It was in Valparaiso, and the girls went to Chesterton schools, which was about a twenty-minute drive for Lisa every morning.

The close quarters for four people led to inevitable arguments and disagreements about almost everything. There was not enough money for the things we needed, the girls didn't like being that far away from school, they did not like sharing a room, there was only one bathroom and very little privacy, and much more.

In "How it Works" in AA, it says that we strive for spiritual progress, not perfection. That is a good way to live any aspect of your life, not just spiritually. Progress is attainable and sustainable. We all tried to feel gratitude in the small things, and that began by looking back. Looking back at where we were recently in housing, finances, stress, and uncertainty gave us more appreciation for what we did have. To this day, I consciously look for the good in all situations. There is some good in every situation, and faith allows us to believe it even if we don't understand it.

The first year back in Valparaiso was still a struggle. True recovery means being able to apply the principles of the twelve steps in real life with all its opportunities for both success and failure. Taking three steps forward and one step back was still much better than before when all it involved was taking steps backward. Alcoholics strive for progress and not perfection. Recovery is a sequence of events, and if knowledge is gained from our mistakes, it always leads to making fewer of them in the future. Lisa and the girls did enjoy not having to live in a basement anymore, and we tried to stay busy and work on enjoying our new normal. We still did beach days and hung out with friends.

That fall I was serving on a team at the Great Banquet and was asked to give a talk and my testimony to the guests there. When I was in my cabin, getting dressed, I said a prayer that I might affect someone who was listening and could relate to my story. I noticed on my way down to the building where the talks were being held that it had started to get overcast after a weekend of beautiful weather.

Before I started talking, I placed a glass of water that was half full on the podium with me. I started my story by explaining that some people thought the glass was half full and some thought it was half empty, but a few short months ago, my glass had been half empty, cracked, and leaking water all over. The notes that I had carefully written were all of a sudden useless because I needed to speak with my heart and not just my voice. My wife and daughters were listening in another room, and I knew that there would be some other people listening who could not comprehend what I was saying and would think differently of me when I was done.

My faith told me that there would also be some people who could relate the way only other alcoholics could, and if I could just reach one, just *one* person, what a blessing it would be. I finished to dead silence and then a loud ovation, but I didn't understand why. I was weak and struggling and had confessed my fallibilities in front of everyone. After the spiritual team members prayed for me, I started back to my cabin to change and was startled when it began to rain lightly. Another baptism? I believe that coincidence is truly God's way of staying anonymous.

Camp Lawrence

Later that weekend, six guests asked if they could speak with me privately, and I believe that I was able to give some hope and clarity to them. Three of those guests, I still see regularly. One man actually did not want help with alcoholism, but when he found out where I worked, he told me that his father worked there and they had a falling out a number of years before. He wanted to know if I would give his father a note when I went back to work. I did, and they had slowly started a relationship again.

Another man was staying at a local halfway house and said that my testimony gave him hope for the future and that he could make it if he took it one day at a time and used his resources.

The final guy is now an active team leader at the Great Banquet and has helped many guests with their own addictions.

There are many things that humanity uses to escape from life, and they are not all bad. What is damaging is the level of the escape. "All things in moderation" should be the mantra for almost everyone. Alcohol, gambling, overeating, video games, social media, and many others can be a distraction and not unhealthy if they are done in moderation and do not negatively affect lives or relationships. In my life, the desire for alcohol has been replaced by the desire to be the best person that I can be.

Step 10 is when we continue to take personal inventory and, when we are wrong, promptly admit it. Nobody is perfect, so I try to stay conscious of what I am doing and saying as it relates to myself and other people. When I promptly admit it, then my wrongs do not add up and overwhelm me and instead provide guidance on staying on the right path.

God says:

> The reason some people have turned against you and walked away from you without reason has nothing to do with you. It is because I have removed them from your life because they cannot go where I am taking you next. They will only hinder you in your next level because they have already served their purpose in your life. Let them go and keep moving. Greater is coming.

This is something I need to always keep in mind, especially during the moments of reflection when my mind likes to glamorize past relationships and make them seem so wonderful and bright, when in reality these past relationships had a lot of darkness and despair. When my mind gets into this place, I must remember to stay in faith and be grateful for the people God has put in my path today. They serve such a wonderful purpose, and if I am busy reflecting on past relationships, then I am missing out on the beauty of new relationships being built around me.

Last Six Years

Hans and Polly...still a man's best friend

Lisa's prayer today and every morning is, "God, thank you for all the blessings, thank you for our family and friends, our jobs, and our health. Please, God, give me a sign of what I need to know today, and bring me peace to live in the moment of today."

Faith is not believing that God can; it's knowing that he will!

Their circumstances worked against them, but they had resilience and faith. They both have very opposite personalities and come from different social backgrounds. They have moved ten times in twenty years and have had a couple of their own businesses and also worked for others. Lisa loves change and new challenges; Hans loves stability and a set schedule. They experience God in different ways and interpret "reality" through different lenses. Yet they have come to appreciate the positives that they bring to each other.

Indiana Dunes Great Banquet

Hannah telling her testimony 2016

Over the last six years, they have stayed close to the Indiana Dunes Great Banquet community and continued to serve as God's disciples as well as invited others as guests to share in God's love. The banquet has been a huge influence in their lives, and they have met many brothers and sisters in Christ whom they would have never met if their journey were different. This community prayed for them, stood in the life gaps, and nourished them through their love.

Their journey also prepared them to keep an eye on God. They had to learn to "let go and let God" in many situations that were not controllable. Rewards and double blessings came from praying and knowing that God would show grace and kindness. They needed to attach to God and not material things. God will provide divine intervention when it is least expected. God gave them a second chance and strength, which they have had the opportunity to share with others.

Faith has given them the patience and understanding to see what others are going through and not have judgment on them. Hans uses his personal knowledge of addiction to help others with counseling or just listening. Lisa's previous anger toward Hans has been replaced by acceptance. Hans knows that he is a much more effective parent and husband if he puts into practice all the twelve steps and repeats them when necessary—not so much to prevent relapse but to remind himself of where he has been. Vigilance and awareness will help keep that devil from the door.

God has a purpose for your pain, a reason for your struggles, and a reward for your faithfulness.

Lisa looks back and realizes that she was fearful of things she didn't understand. Fear can drive stress and anxiety. It can play havoc on your mental health. She reacted to fear because she wanted to know what was going to happen and needed so badly to control things.

Over time the realization that she had no control but God did has given her peace of mind. She needed to be quiet, listen, and be willing to accept where the process would lead her family. She needed to do a lot of self-talk during the dark times. She reminded herself that she was enough, was loved, had a purpose, and had the strength that she didn't even know she had and that there was a reason for this season. Rehashing the past is not healthy and will not do any good.

Fear nothing and pray about everything. Be strong, trust God's Word, and know that God desires for our lives to be like fruitful branches of a grapevine. The only way to be fruitful is to remain connected to Jesus, the vine, and allow God to be the gardener to prune our lives and to stimulate growth and fruitfulness. It is God's cultivating, weeding, and pruning in our life that brings forth spiritual fruit, character development, and good fruit in mankind. Just as nourishment for the desired fruit comes through the vine, so does the fullness of life come through faith in Jesus Christ.

They need to stay close to Jesus, the source of power. He has grown them and loved them. Stay close to him, and have faith that he has a better plan than we have for ourselves. We are not the Savior, but we can love others as he loves us.

Lisa used to think that her life was so different from her friends or acquaintances. Just because people can't see the hurt and chaos doesn't mean they aren't going through something. She had several friends throughout the years who only knew a little of the struggle the family was going through.

Both Hans and Lisa went into marriage deeply wounded and full of pain. Hans numbed his pain through alcohol, and Lisa numbed hers through control. Her pain was so deep that she didn't trust him, and it compromised her relationship with others. Unless the hurt is dealt with when it occurs, it will accumulate.

Lisa's parents didn't know how to deal with the hurt. Time rarely heals anything. Pain gets deeper, and it doesn't go away. Everyone deals with pain in a unique way—right or wrong. It will come out somewhere. Let go and let God. Our emotions only heal when it comes through the presence of others and God. The only way to stop the hurt and totally resolve it is to turn it over to God. Emotional pain almost destroyed their marriage. God needed to heal their hearts and turn the pain toward him. They needed to learn to be honest before God. They lived with Satan for so long—full of fear and shame.

If you hide from God, you hide from the healer. Pain will manifest itself until it is given to God. We all need to get quiet with the Lord and be responsible to God. Our response to life forms us. We need to forgive ourselves because God forgave us first.

Sometimes you need to do what is best for you and not what is best for others.

Regret focuses on the past. The cross is about the future. Hans and Lisa needed to learn from the past and let go. God says, "Love your enemies, bless those who curse you, and do good to those who hate you." We need to depend on the Holy Spirit. Pain needs to be forced out of our heads into our hearts so that we can forgive. Forgiveness comes from the heart, and it is healing.

The Holy Spirit is healing and will fill us up and make us healthy. We need to depend on the Holy Spirit for emotional healing and health, joy, love, peace, patience, gentleness, and self-control. God removed all lies, worthlessness, emotional failure, rejection, and betrayal. He takes away the old message and gives you a new message. The devil is the hurt-whisperer.

Romans 12:2 says "that the only way to know what God thinks is best for you is to not let your thinking be conformed to the world. Then you will be able to see the renewing of the mind, which is a change of heart and life." Both Hans and Lisa had hard hearts and needed them softened. They were transformed by God's truth and not the truth of mankind. Jesus truly speaks to everyone like he did his disciples. He said, "I will never leave you or forsake you. I will help you through this mess." Jesus took them, wrapped them in his arms, and stayed with them through it all.

Alcoholism is a chronic disease of the brain.

One of the things they are so grateful for is that regardless of the pain of walking or trying to sprint through the nightmare, their daughters knew that alcoholism was hereditary and could run in their family. They have been very fortunate to have a pediatrician who knew the story and had shared with the girls the importance of not self-medicating to cover up pain. Both Hannah and Delaney have a low tolerance for any kind of pain, and the pediatricians had been more than supportive of educating them.

Someone once told Lisa that dealing with a disease such as alcoholism is like going through the process of grieving the loss of a loved one. These are the stages of grieving:

1. **Denial.** Your world becomes meaningless and overwhelming. Life does not make sense, and there is disbelief that the life that was dreamed of was being shattered. You have to simply take each day at a time and deal with whatever comes your way.

2. **Anger.** At first, Lisa was angry at Hans for allowing alcohol to take over his life and ruin their family. Then she learned that it wasn't Hans; it was the disease she hated so much that was taking over the man she loved. She just wanted Hans back to normal.

3. **Bargaining.** Lisa tried to plead with Hans not to drink. She tried to tell him she could make it better. If only he didn't drink, then life would look like this or that. There was a lot of negotiating with Hans—or she thought was Hans. But more likely, it was the disease.

4. **Depression.** It is hard not to go through this stage. There was a feeling of emptiness. Lisa asked herself, "How am I going to raise the girls alone?" She didn't sign up to be a single parent. The girls didn't sign up to live in a family with such dysfunction.

5. **Acceptance.** There came a time when their family needed to learn to accept the disease and the effect it had on the family. They needed to learn to live with it. It was the new "normal." Once they learned to accept the new normal, there started to be better days. They could live again and enjoy their lives. They started to grow, learn, and evolve into people they liked. They now invest in themselves and friendships. There was a time that they lived in isolation, but today they live in real time. Things are handled as they come along.

Hans and Lisa have different resources they use to get through the recovery process. She loves reading, educating herself, and finding gratitude. Hans loves coffee time with his friends, being a recovery coach and going to AA meetings. They both have learned that each way of recovery is different, and they need to appreciate it.

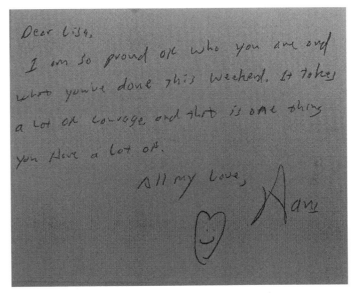

Note from Hans to Lisa

Be so confident about God's plan that you don't even get upset when things don't work out!

A strong faith can relieve you from having expectations in return for your deeds. Just knowing that the good they do now will come back to them many times over is sustaining. Hans was asked to give a testimonial of his life's story to other men at the Indiana Dunes Great Banquet men's retreat. Since that day, there have been a reconciliation with parents, years of sobriety, and one guest is an addiction recovery coach. All from men who were inspired when they heard his talk. Hans made everyone proud for taking his story which God had given him, and sharing it with others who might be going through some of the same life issues, fighting an addiction without knowing where to turn. Hans was humble as he told his story, and there were many of our brothers and sisters who knew a little of what was going on but really not to the extent of what had happened. Hannah and Delaney both attended Hans's talk and probably heard some things for the first time. The girls know this is their story as well, and it is what has helped mold them into who they are today.

Hans and Lisa have been very active in helping people that they see who are in need. They have learned that God wants them to be the hands and feet for others. All along the journey, they have always made sure to prioritize giving back together and individually. Serving meals at the homeless shelter or for Meals on Wheels, singing Christmas carols at the nursing home, donating essentials to the shelters, taking up food and clothing donations, and whatever else presents itself.

The girls also give back as Hannah served on a mission trip during her first spring break at college. She traveled to North Carolina and rebuilt homes for hurricane victims. Delaney tutors students and helps mothers with young children. Hannah and Delaney had a friend who wanted to stay in the area for summer break from college in 2018 but did not have a place to live. Hannah asked if she could spend the summer with the family, and she would share her room with her. Hans and Lisa were glad and blessed that they could have her stay with them for the summer.

They have made it a new tradition to give back to one organization or cause a month because they have been provided for by others, and it is God's will to do the same for those around them. Whether it's giving extra change to the bell ringers at the holidays, making tie blankets for people in hospice, or delivering Thanksgiving meals for Meals on Wheels, mankind is here on earth to be the hands and feet of Jesus for others.

> *This is my commandment, that you love one another as I have loved you.*
>
> —*John 15:12*

Love goes beyond mere words. Sometimes it is spoken silence when we don't condemn someone who comes looking for help. The Schellers had many people placed by God who knew their story and still loved them unconditionally. During this time, they learned that apart from God and others, we can't love one another selflessly as God intended. God is patient, and we need to grow in Christ. It is a journey, not a destination. Sometimes we need to reflect on God's grace in order to give us confidence in the future. God's slowness is his grace, mercy, and patience toward all of us. Give your heart to God, and you won't be able to contain your love for others.

Recovery isn't black or white, right or wrong, or 100 percent in any direction, which is where Hans and Lisa were stuck at. It was frustrating for Lisa because Hans couldn't see things outside the box. She had her ideas on how things should be and was micromanaging and correcting everything. They came to realize that recovery was about balance and integration. They had to learn to meet each other where they were and not where they thought each other should be.

Hans as certified peer recovery coach

Hans has slowly worked himself into the recovery community in Porter County. He regularly attends AA meetings but has volunteered for other agencies, such as Recovery Connection, Frontline Foundations, and Artistic Recovery. When Hans was a soccer coach, he was a big proponent of showing the players what to do instead of just telling them what to do. He felt that doing something showed them that he had done exactly what he was asking them to do. The fact that he had not just read about or studied it but actually did it lends credibility. When Hans sponsors or counsels someone in recovery, they know that he has felt most of the same feelings, emotions, and struggles they are having. There is only patience, caring, acceptance, and understanding.

There was a time where Lisa wanted Hans to really believe in God and know that, if we surrendered to him, God would take care of their problems. Lisa bought books for Hans to read, sent him Bible verses, asked him to pray about it, and invited guys who were friends from church over to talk to him. Lisa always saw one foot in and one foot out with Hans. Today it is not like that at all. Hans is a true believer and knows he wouldn't be where he is today without God's grace and mercy.

After months of praying for God to use him and his journey, in December 2019, Hans was offered a position with Recovery Connection and now is a certified peer recovery coach and is using this life experience to help others understand and overcome their issues with addiction.

In January 2021, Lisa received her national certification as a recovery family coach, nutrition coach, relapse coach, as well as a life coach.

They feel incredibly blessed that their daughters have come through their turbulent times as loving, caring, compassionate, and gracious young women. By God's grace, they have stayed together in clear commitment to each other and to God and have discovered that staying power resides in God's commitment to us and our surrender to that commitment. Ultimately, their resiliency resulted from their response to the gift that God has given them as individuals, as a couple, and as a family.

It is easier to stay doing what you have done because you know the outcome, it is comfortable no matter the situation, and changing is harder. Most people won't change until the pain of staying the same is worse than the pain of changing. Today their lives are so much different because Hans chooses life over alcohol.

Life is good

In this house, our family does second chances. We give grace, we are real, we make mistakes, we say "I am sorry," we make life loud, we give hugs, we make family, we pray together, we have faith and sure do love!

By God's grace, their family has stayed together in clear commitment to each other and to our God. They have discovered that staying power resides in God's commitment and surrender to that commitment. Ultimately, the staying power resulted in a response to the gift that God has given as individuals, as a couple, and as a family.

There were many situations they faced that seemed to be enough to allow the differences to drive a wedge between them. However, it has been a huge outpouring of God's grace for them to stay together as a family. It is a deliberate choice to stay together as a family. If Hans and Lisa had wanted to separate, they could have found many reasons to do so, but they chose not to and found enough reasons to stay together. The circumstances they have faced thus far have brought them closer together. Also, their choice to stay united has to do with the choice to put faith in God and let him guide them. God has blessed them to be a strong family and has added his protection over them.

They have dealt with many stressful life changes—such as divorce, marital separation, imprisonment, death of parents, personal injury or illness, marriage, dismissal from work, marital reconciliation, moving, and daughters leaving home—and have come through it all even stronger.

You must learn a new way to think before you can master a new way to be. Hans and Lisa needed to set new healthy boundaries.

Hans needs his space to develop his own relationships and friendships. Friends are a big part of his life now, and he needs to wind down at the end of the day to work out and read as a distraction from the day's events. Hans needs structure and mentally thrives with it. His gratitude and humility are reflected with a positive attitude, and they remind Lisa on a daily basis where they have been, how far they have come, and how much better their lives are today.

Lisa is much calmer about things today and doesn't get uptight about the little things or worry as much. Knowing that Hans has a life outside of her makes her happy. God has really been a presence in their life. The greatest gift Hans and Lisa have given Hannah and Delaney is their own recovery. The second gift is to give the girls a chance to do their own healing. They are very open about alcoholism with the girls, and they, too, are open with them.

Whether it's having coffee with someone, attending an Al-Anon meeting, being available when people call, or helping them make a new resource connection, they feel so blessed to help those who are struggling or don't know where to turn.

Today Lisa doesn't worry about where Hans is, what he is doing, or how he spends his time or money. She doesn't worry whether or not he is being honest, if he is attending the AA meeting he said he was going to, or if he is really at work.

They reflect and wonder, "Do people really know our story? Have they walked a mile in our shoes? Do they have our best interest?"

God gave them this life, and they would not trade it for anything. It has taught them so much about their parents, upbringing, siblings, themselves, as well as their relationship with others. They are much better people today because of their family journey. People need to know that this disease can affect anyone, and just as with other diseases, knowing what you are dealing with is the best way to start the recovery process. There is power in sharing your story. Faith is what got them through hardships and what gives them tangible solutions.

Adjusting and acknowledging each other's triggers was crucial. You can't control a situation, but you can contribute to it, either positively or negatively. Lisa knows that she is one of Hans's triggers, and it is her reaction toward Hans that may decide how things are going to turn out.

Having family fun

Girls and Lisa

22 years!
Very BLESSED &
GRATEFUL!!! ♥

2019-2021 Lisa and Hans

Over the last six years, their family has progressively had to adjust, heal, and learn a new normal as they navigated recovery. Not only Hans's sobriety and recovery but the entire family's recovery. Hans and Lisa were not exactly sure what that was going to look like. They had to set new boundaries and routines and try not to relapse into the old habits they were so accustomed to for survival before Hans left.

The family understands that recovery is a journey and not a destination. There is no instant solution or quick fix like everyone so desperately wants. They have all had to work on themselves and give each other the space and grace to do just that. New habits of gratitude, positivity, commitment, joyfulness, and humility had to be learned. A couple of Hans's favorite sayings are "Everyone needs to have a WHY in their lives" and "One day at a time."

Lisa and Hans 20th Anniversary

Twenty years together.

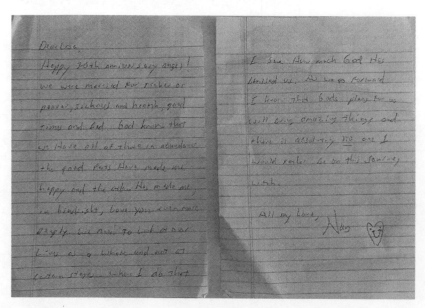

Happy 20th

As of the fall of 2021, Hans and Lisa have been married for twenty-two years. Both Hannah and Delaney have graduated from high school and attend Valparaiso University. Hannah is a senior and will be graduating May 2022 with an elementary education degree, and Delaney is a sophomore with a desire to major in psychology.

The girls did not have a normal upbringing, but God has blessed them with a village of Christian people who have helped raise the girls and have been truly an extension of God's grace. He has blessed them in ways that could never have been imagined ten years ago. They needed to go through the struggle to understand that we all serve an amazing God. He put many people in their lives to help be the hands and feet. It is an extension of his kindness and a reflection of his love for us. God wants us all to do the same for others, no matter how hard it may be, because the blessings received are much greater than what we can give ourselves.

The Son of God said, "I did not come to be served but to serve others." If we are not meeting the needs of others, our lives become meaningless.

Over the last six years, they have come to realize that God has always provided. It didn't matter if they lived in a five-thousand-square-foot house, a hotel, or someone's basement—they always had food, shelter, clothing, and love. The girls never went without. By living a simpler lifestyle, now they can relax and enjoy more things. They have become less materialistic, put quality over quantity, and now value things that give them peace—not chasing the American dream or societal expectations. They live more mindfully and more intentionally and try to find gratitude every day, appreciating life's small pleasures and embracing the white space.

Hans's 60ᵗʰ Birthday

The major downsize over the last six years has been eliminating their four storage units. For ten years they stored what was thought to be their most valued possessions. Moving as often as they did after living in our five-thousand-square-foot house, they put belongings in storage three times. Not just one storage unit but four large storage units. They lived without these belongings for ten years—things that were inherited from Hans's parents, both sets of grandparents, and Lisa's mom. These were things they thought were needed to fill the void. During the ten-year period, realization set in that these were material things that weren't seen or made a difference in everyday life. Little by little, things were sold or given away. They are now down to one storage unit and live very comfortably.

When there are arguments now, it is mostly because of the lack of communication. Lisa chooses to walk away, go into the bedroom, and take a deep breath but still gets irritated and sometimes says things she would later regret. Communication is the key now in disagreements. Things are talked out, and they both say that this is a *big* plus in the marriage.

Now when there is an argument in the family, they both try to always look at the big picture and how insignificant what they are arguing about is. Realization of what they are doing and it is not who they are. It calms the situation quickly, and patience is the by-product of it.

As a family, there are still issues. Whenever "self" gets involved, then problems start to arise. When someone wants something, it can lead to the exclusion of other things. Life is full of trade-offs, and the decisions made should reflect the family needs as opposed to individual needs.

Tense moments exist at times. Disagreements lead to silent treatments and unhappiness. Differences in personalities and human selfishness cause hurts and even tears. They are not the perfect family. Sometimes tolerance is very thin, and the respect is not there, which causes conflict.

"If I could give my girls . . ."

They are very proud of Hannah and Delaney for all they have overcome. Both girls were very fortunate to have been in the show choir throughout high school. Hannah and Delaney were both two-year captains. They were strong leaders, caring and determined. They always gave 100 percent. It was their release. Delaney was named outstanding performer multiple times. Both girls led their show choir teams to nationals while supported by a wonderful community of friends, and the traveling opportunities they had shaped them into the young ladies they are today.

Girls at Valparaiso University 2020

Family Fun Camping

Both Hannah and Delaney started school at Valparaiso University with an excellent Twenty-First Century Scholarship and academic scholarships from the Indiana Twenty-First Century Scholarship Program. While Hans was sick and not working, they relied on Lisa's salary, which wasn't much. They were at a barbecue with some friends and got into a discussion about the girls and their future education. One of Lisa's friends was in a similar situation, and she asked about the Twenty-First Century Scholarship Program. Based on their income, the girls would qualify for the program. Lisa filled out the paperwork when the girls were both in eighth grade. If they did the four assignments each high school year, they would qualify for the scholarship. This has been one of the greatest blessings during the journey.

Hannah and Delaney are very different. The girls give Hans and Lisa strength.

Hannah is "Look out, world, here I come." She has a very strong personality and is a leader who doesn't worry about what others think. Delaney is sensitive and emotional. She worries and feels for others. Both girls talk openly about their dad's disease. It is not a secret. Both girls have told their stories at teen church retreats. They are open to talking to anyone about it to help make a difference. The girls see many blessings that have come out of their lives.

Both Hannah and Delaney have learned that you never know whom you will encounter in life that has or is fighting the same battle.

> *They say it takes a village to raise a child, and I, Lisa, want to say thank you to my "village"!*
> *I had many village mommas who helped raise our girls . . . They prayed for us, watched over us, and loved us unconditionally. Thank you from the bottom of my heart. Love you all! Lisa*

The girls knew they always had a village of moms that they could contact in a time of a crisis if things got really bad or they needed someone to talk to. They participated in activities that made themselves confident and happy, and both of them stayed close to friends. The girls knew who their close friends were and where the safe places were that they could go when they felt things were out of control.

The girls are Hans and Lisa's everything. Their childhood was far from perfect, but they experienced things that not many children ever experience, and these have shaped them forever. One out of every four children comes from an addictive home, so Hans and Lisa wanted so much to protect the girls. It is common knowledge that children are like sponges and soak up everything in their environment. They are watching us as parents, for we are their first teachers. They mimic us and act out what they mirror us doing. Life with Hans was a drama. Just because the girls were quiet at times didn't mean they weren't paying attention or didn't know there was a problem. The girls had a much deeper understanding than they shared.

There is a poem that reads:

> One hundred years from now, it won't matter—my bank account, the house I lived in, the car I drove. But what will matter is the difference I made in a child's life.

Lisa's prayer for her girls is to make sure that they know how much they are loved and that they have a family to come home to.

As part of their family's recovery, they needed to educate themselves about the disease and process it. They needed to reclaim their own lives and do for themselves instead of being consumed with Hans's disease and also learn to trust Hans again. Trust took a big toll on the relationship. And Lisa needed to know that Hans's actions aligned with his words and that he did what he said he was doing. Starting afresh and removing all the negative things from the past was crucial. The entire family had to decide what mattered the most—such as honesty, God, and family time. The phrase "Detach with love." They all had to learn that even though they loved each other very much, they were not responsible for the choices of another person and were very powerless over addiction. They know that recovery is a lifelong process.

You are the average of the five people you surround yourself with—they truly believe this. When Hans and Lisa began struggling, they were surrounding themselves with critical, negative, and unhappy people. They became like those people. Then Hans and Lisa acted that way to each other. As they started to open their lives to others and let them in, small changes started to occur, and the new friends started to shape their lives, attitudes, and behavior. They had to get out of their negative environment to see all the opportunities that God had for them. Hans and Lisa now find themselves among people who hold them accountable and at higher standards. Socialization is with those people, and it makes Hans and Lisa better people. They were not always setting a positive example for the girls, and they picked up on a lot of negativity. Sometimes God removes people from situations—toxic people and places—because that is a part of his plan. You may think that everything is falling apart, but actually, everything is falling into place.

Respect is another important reason that fuels their commitment to stay together. Opinions are respected, and they show respect; it is given back twofold.

Tolerance is the capacity to endure pain or hardship. No family can stay together without a high degree of tolerance. Pain and hardships affect every family. Hans and Lisa's tolerance became very high with what was thrown at them over the years.

There's nothing wrong with expressing your needs or views, and every family has their viewpoints and how they see many situations differently. On the contrary, this indicates a healthy family relationship. Demanding that your needs be a priority and imposing your views creates stress, and many families experience testing beyond what they can withstand. Everyone wants to have a voice at times. Lisa thought early on in the marriage that she knew what was best for both of them and wanted so much to have control. It backfired, and she needed to learn to let Hans have a voice in our decisions instead of just going along.

You can fool people outside of your home for a long period of time, but those closest to you can see the real you. Being authentic now inspires trust among the members of their family. If you trust someone, you want to talk to them and share your secrets with them. Authentic relationships foster trust, and trust is the foundational material for good relationships.

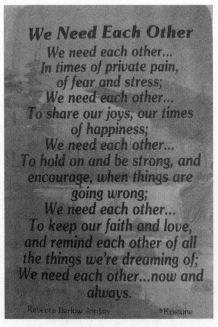

We Need Each Other

We need each other...
In times of private pain,
of fear and stress;
We need each other...
To share our joys, our times
of happiness;
We need each other...
To hold on and be strong, and
encourage, when things are
going wrong;
We need each other...
To keep our faith and love,
and remind each other of all
the things we're dreaming of;
We need each other...now and
always.

Rebecca Barlow Jordan   ®Kristone

We need each other

Papa loved watching the girls Show Choir

Papa giving Hannah and Delaney wise advice

Summer 2018

Families that play together stay together—not only play but "do stuff" together. Their family loves together time, doing things like playing games, watching movies, going on day excursions, and going out to dinner. They work the business together and love going to church together and so much more. Looking over the years, they remind the girls that the family has been so blessed. The girls have never gone without even through it all.

Disagreements lead to silent treatments and unhappiness. Differences in personalities and human selfishness cause hurts and even tears. It is not laughter all the time, and they are not the perfect family. Sometimes tolerance is very thin and respect is not there.

> *Grace is when God provides us good things that we may not deserve.*
> *Mercy is when he spares us from bad things we may deserve.*
> *Blessings are when God is generous with both.*
> *God is good all the time!*

They believe this is all God's grace. Somehow, their family became the place where God decided to grow all the parts they did not have in and of themselves. They individually and collectively chose God, and he made sure that all the necessary pieces were there for keeping them together, slowly developing over the years and now being transmitted to the next generation through the children.

June 2018 was Hannah's high school graduation party, which was outside in the backyard. Lisa was worried about having it there because of the limited space, but Hannah said, "Don't worry, Mom, it will work out."

At an open house, people don't RSVP, so you have no idea how many people to expect. The day came. Many tents were popped up in the backyard. The girls decorated and got the food out. People started to arrive. Then at one point, while they were talking to friends, Lisa looked out among the people, and the tears started to roll down her face. After all that they had been through, the number of people who came to celebrate was unbelievable.

There were people from all walks. There were friends from before the girls were born; there were elementary, middle school, and high school teachers of Hannah's; there were neighbors they met when they lived in the half-million-dollar house. There were friends from when they lived in a basement, church friends from all the churches they attended, Great Banquet friends, show choir parents and kids, work friends, old neighbors, friends who have been there for over twenty years, friends who have been a huge part of recovery, and new friends they met along their journey.

They were in awe. Over 350 people came to celebrate Hannah. The feelings of love, peace, and joy were overwhelming. God knows the people that are needed in their lives both yesterday, today, and tomorrow. They realized on this day that these people didn't have to come to her party; they came because they wanted to. "Overwhelmingly blessed" was the only emotion to describe how God put all these amazing people in their lives to guide and help mold Hannah and Delaney into who they are today. They all stepped into the gap that addiction had created and filled that void with love.

Hannah's High School Graduation

God had a way to show them seasonal and permanent people because some have been fair-weather and only were friends if it served them a purpose. Some of them became very judgmental and decided that their circumstances were not what they wanted to be a part of or didn't fit with their beliefs. But many have been open and compassionate and showed grace and mercy. Exactly how blessed they have been became very clear with Hannah's high school graduation's open house.

Family, 2020

Thanksgiving 2020

COVID-19 and its resulting restrictions changed the way Hans and Lisa lived, as it did for everyone. Places they could go, things they could do, and even people that they could see. It made a lot of people angry, but everything in life has more than one perspective. People were upset that they could not go to church. Faith and God are not in a building but in your heart, and nobody or nothing can take that away. Restaurants were closed, so it was an opportunity to become closer as a family by sharing meals together. Delaney's show choir group had already qualified for nationals again when the rest of the season was canceled. Everyone was disappointed but understood why it happened.

Giving Back

The next major thing that was impacted was Delaney's graduation and open house. A car parade through town and then diplomas given at the high school were done instead of the typical pomp and circumstance at the football field. It was a huge success. A friend let them use an open-top Jeep, and they saw many people they knew lined up along the parade route. The alternative would have been sitting on metal bleachers for three hours in ninety-degree heat. They decided to do Delaney's open house with social distancing in the backyard. Lisa's sister and her family came in from Minnesota as the travel was not very restrictive yet.

The day came with a forecast of rain, but it was decided to go ahead with it anyway. The tent canopies were set up, and the rest was in God's hands. He would decide how it would play out. And the weather truly would not make or break the joy and love of the event. There were many who could not attend due to COVID restrictions, but they still prayed for Delaney and sent her texts, phone calls, and cards. The unconditional love was so amazing.

Delaney's High School Graduation

As our family looks back at the entire tapestry of our lives, we can see from the perspective of the present moment that every aspect of our lives was necessary and perfect. Each step eventually led to a higher place, even though these steps often felt like obstacles or painful experiences.

—*Paraphrased from a quote by Wayne Dyer*

God expects you to use your pain to help others. Whatever mistake, failure, trouble, trial, or bad decisions you have experienced, God says, "I'll still use it for good in your life. And I expect you to use it to help others."

What We Have Learned

Be the change you wish to see in the world!

Lisa

I have learned the following:
1. God truly does an amazing job with broken people.
2. Faith isn't asking God to stop the storm. Faith is about trusting God to help you through the storm.
3. Sometimes a miracle is simply meeting someone with a good heart.
4. When you finally learn that a person's behavior has more to do with their own internal struggle than it ever did with you, you learn *grace*.
5. "Trust the Lord with all your heart and lean not on your own understanding; in all your ways submit to Him, and He will make your paths straight" (Proverbs 3:5–6).
6. Always pray to have eyes that see the best, a heart that forgives the worst, a mind that forgets the bad, and a soul that never loses faith.
7. At some point, you just have to let go of what you thought should happen and live in what is happening.
8. I have two angels watching over me, and I call them Mom and Dad.
9. Amazing things happen when you distance yourself from negativity and toxicity.
10. Don't forget, you may be the only lighthouse in someone else's storm.
11. Friendship isn't about who you've known the longest. It's the person who showed up and said, "I'm here for you," and stuck by you through everything—my "village mommas."

12. Learn to trust the journey even when you do not understand it. Sometimes what you never wanted or expected turns out to be what you needed.

13. I am proud of the woman I am today because I went through one hell of a time becoming her.

14. No one escapes being wounded. We are all wounded people.

15. It's funny because we ask God to change our situation, not knowing he put us in the situation to change us.

16. One reason people resist change is that they focus on what they must give up instead of what they might gain.

17. All that I need to know at any given time is revealed to me. I trust myself, and I trust life.

18. You win in marriage by losing the selfish desire to get out of your own way. Talk and work together instead of fighting.

19. One day you'll find someone who chooses you and continues to choose you every day, and that's when you will be thankful that everything happened the way it did.

20. We cannot control others; they must walk their own journey.

21. Peace is the result of retraining your mind to process life as it is rather than it should be.

22. You were given this life because God knew before you were born that you were strong enough to live it.

23. People won't always see things as you do. Let it go! You won't always see things as others do. Let it go!

24. No matter where you are on your journey, it is exactly where you are supposed to be.

25. The reason we struggle with insecurity is that we compare our behind-the-scenes life with everyone else's highlight reel.

26. If you feed your confidence, you will starve your fear.

27. Everyone has a past. The past does not equal the future unless you live there.

28. Ego says, "Once everything falls into place, I will find peace." Spirit says, "Find peace, and everything will fall into place."

29. Your storms are only temporary; your blessings are forever.
30. You are not defined by someone's opinion.
31. Life sucks, but what was your lesson or gift?
32. Unconditional love means no judgment and no shame.
33. Life isn't happening to you but for you.
34. You have choices, and we get to decide. Nothing is wasted.
35. Gratitude is one of our greatest blessings.
36. God has a purpose for our lives. I am not married to the same person; we relearn each other.
37. God will lead us if we follow. God gave us tools and courage and accountability.
38. God took us to something and restored us for the better and redemption.
39. God would not release me from my marriage.
40. Marriage vows are for sickness and health, richer or poorer.
41. I am much stronger in our relationship.
42. God left the ninety-nine for the one.
43. "God is our refuge and our only strength" (Psalm 46–1).
44. God offers redemption.
45. God will slowly take everything away.
46. You cannot go back in time.
47. We have countless stories of blessings.
48. God can bring us through all things and bring us good.
49. The beautiful thing about life is that you can always change, grow, and get better. You are not defined by your past. You are not your mistakes.
50. God renewed our life and blessed us by rebuilding it.
51. God restores everything.
52. I trust God's plan, not mine.
53. Live one day at a time.
54. "Everything little thing is going to be all right" (Bob Marley).
55. Nobody escapes from being wounded.
56. God knew what he was doing.
57. No matter where we are on our journey of life, it is exactly where we are supposed to be.

58. God's grace is the love and mercy given to us by God because God desires us to have it, not necessarily because of anything we have done to earn it.

God's Beauty

I asked God for strength, that I might achieve,
I was made weak, that I might learn to be humble to obey.
I asked for health, that I might do greater things,
I was given infirmity, that I might do better things.
I asked for riches, that I might be happy,
I was given poverty, that I might be wise.
I asked for power, that I might have the praise of people,
I was given weakness, that I might feel the need of God.
I asked for all things, that I might enjoy life,
I was given life, that I might enjoy all things.
I got nothing that I asked for
but everything I had hoped for.
Almost despite myself,
my unspoken prayers were answered.
I am among all people, most richly blessed.
Anonymous

Lisa and Michele

Colleen and Lisa

Lisa and Jeanne Ann

* * *

<u>Quotes</u>

In order to love who you are, you cannot hate the experiences that shaped you.

Gratitude unlocks the fullness of life. It turns what we have into enough, and more. It turns denial into acceptance, chaos in order, and confusion into clarity. It turns a meal into a feast, a house into a home, a stranger into a friend. Gratitude makes sense of our past, brings peace to today, and creates a vision for tomorrow.
—Melody Beattie

May you have the courage to break the patterns that no longer serve you.

God is saying to you: "My child, you are worrying too much. Remember who I am. There is nothing too hard for me. You may not see it, but I have everything planned out for you."

Dear Mom, because of you, I am who I am today. Thank you! I love you! George.

Pay attention to your patterns. The ways you learned to survive may or may not be the ways you want to continue to live. Heal and shift.

I will trust and not be afraid.
—Isaiah 12:2

Life is a proving ground for us. God sent us to earth to learn and grow through experiences, both pleasant and painful. He lets us choose between good and evil and lets us decide whether we will serve others or focus on ourselves. The challenge is to have faith in HIS plan even though we don't have all of the answers. Because we all make mistakes, God sent his Son, Jesus Christ, so we can be cleansed and forgiven. When we accept Jesus and follow HIS example, we become less selfish and enjoy greater love, peace, and joy.

Love isn't a state of perfect caring. It is an active noun like "struggle." To love someone is to strive to accept that person exactly the way he or she is, here and now.

—Fred Rogers

Put God first, and watch your life change.

God will always provide. It just may be different than what we had in mind.

When you forgive, you heal. When you let go, you grow.

Now, every time I witness a strong person, I want to know: What darkness did you conquer in your story? Mountains do not rise without earthquakes.

As we go through life, we start to understand that it's not important to have a lot of friends. What truly matters is that we have real friends.

The opposite of faith is not doubt, the opposite of faith is control.

—Richard Rohr

They say it takes a village to raise a child, and I just want to say thank you to my "village." If you have watched, loved, or prayed for our child, thank you from the bottom of our hearts!

The journey of reclamation produced a revolution in my soul, a divine turning point that moved me from merely surviving to thriving.

A lot of things broke my heavy heart but fixed my vision.

Our greatest glory is not never failing, but in rising up every time we fail.
—Ralph Waldo Emerson

Never be afraid to fall apart because it is an opportunity to rebuild yourself the way you wish you had been all along.

I will forever remain humble because I know I could have less.

I will forever be grateful because I have had less.

God always knows exactly what we need to hear: "Have I not commanded you? Be strong and courageous. Do not be frightened, and do not be dismayed, for the Lord your God is with you wherever you go" (Joshua 1:9).

Be humble and kind.
—Tim McGraw

Do you know how many times the enemy has tried to kill you? But you are still here by the grace of God.

A child's shoulders were not built to bear the weight of their parents' choices.

The road I traveled hasn't been easy, but I am still here. The only reason I am still here today is because God was walking this road with me, every step of the way.

God loves us in the spaces where we can't possibly love or accept ourselves. That is the beauty and miracle of grace.

Never be a prisoner of your past. It was just a lesson, not a life sentence.

When you finally learn a person's behavior has more to do with their own internal struggle than it ever did with you . . . you learn grace.

Be grateful to everyone.

Faith is all about believing you don't know how it will happen but you know it will.

It's funny because we ask God to change our situation not knowing he put us in the situation to change us.

If you always do what you've always done, you'll always get what you have always gotten.

A miracle is a shift in perception from fear to love.

No matter how many steps you have taken away from God, it only takes one step to get back! Do not turn down God's grace and mercy.

5 Things to Quit
1. Trying to please everyone
2. Fearing change
3. Living in the past
4. Putting yourself down
5. Overthinking

Your circle should want you to win. Your circle should clap the loudest when you have good news. If they don't, get a new circle.

Stay in the moment.

Anyone can find the dirt in someone. Be the one who finds the gold.

I have been a depressed mom. A sad mom. A happy mom. A mean mom. A drained mom. A broken mom. A stable mom. An unstable mom. But I have tried my best to be there, no matter what!

We don't meet people by accident. They are meant to cross our path for a reason.

No matter what anyone thinks of me, God knows my heart, and that is all that matters.

The best part of life? Every morning you have a new opportunity to become a better version of yourself.

* * *

I, Lisa, knew in my heart that I could no longer walk with Hans down his path of sin. There was a deep sadness because I loved Hans. I needed to release him with a loving heart. Jesus understood because he is the only one that could soften Hans's heart. It was not my battle to fight. I needed to depend and rely on the power of the Holy Spirit.

When a marriage is about to self-destruct, it is not because of the hurt but because of the unforgiveness. It's not the hurt but the refusal to forgive that destroys a marriage. No one ever feels like forgiving, but we do it because it is the right thing to do, and you do it to get on with life. This was not an easy task for me, but with God's power, I could move on.

Lisa and her sister Sheila

Lisa and her Dad. Lisa's Dad passed away 2/17/2020 from AML

* * *

Quotes

Have the courage to live a life true to yourself, not the life you expect.

God and my girlfriends are always there for me.

God knits, shapes, and molds us.

God rescues us from our shame and guilt with forgiveness, redemption, and deep love.

We need to be a child of conviction.

When does the soul show up?
—Psalm 151

Have an attitude of gratitude.

Give encouragement—we are all in this together.

Sometimes it takes a tragedy to bring us back to God.

Setbacks are scary and uncertain, but it can be a wakeup call:
How much we need God.
How much we need the Gospel and Good News.

God is in control—be still.

Life is full of peaks and valleys. Climb the mountain.

You will not be troubled—"but take heart, for I have overcome the world" (John 16:33).

Daily prayer:
Please, God, show me a sign you are there.

It's okay to be messed up, but don't stay there.

He showed me grace so that I could be saved.
Because God loves me, he made me broken.
God is going to renovate everything to make it new.
Sin comes out in the open and loses power.
We are all a hot mess.

Pay attention to the environment we are cultivating.
The seed is the Word of God.
The soil is our heart.

The Hope we have in Jesus shapes and changes our lives.

Faith is believing something is true. We can't pass faith on to someone else. God plants it in their hearts.

God asks us to do things that are difficult.

Keep doing the last thing consistently and faithfully.

Thank you for opening doors and pushing me through.

God's plan is always better.

Stay consistent, and don't get discouraged.

Prove to God you are faithful.

The Holy Spirit will grip our sin.

Expect that God can intervene.

People need to be reminded and not instructed.

Sometimes we need to look back on God's grace in order to give us confidence in the future.

God's slowness is actually his grace, his mercy, and his patience toward us.

God will preserve you, and he will be patient.

The Christian life is a journey.

Fruit grows over time with repentance, obedience, and love for one another.

In the midst of tragedy for children:
- Nothing will take away the pain and suffering your children have encountered.
- Try to keep a routine as much as possible.
- Let your children know you are there for them.
- Have fun with your children—keep them involved.
- Tell your children that their emotions are valuable.
- Accept your child's emotions as they are.
- Discuss the situation with your child; be honest without obsessing.
- Let your child ask questions at a deeper level.
- Without scaring them, tell your children that pain and hurt do happen in the world.

- Help your child to take a step back from tragedy.
- Understand that your child may have lost trust in you.

* * *

Songs That Resonate with Me about Our Journey

"Living on a Prayer" by Bon Jovi reminds me of Hans and me. We were two middle-class people who made it through love and ambition by living on a prayer. Hans told me earlier on in our relationship to take his hand and promised we would make it. Being reminded of his promise, I needed to give it my all. God saw us through.

"Ocean"
Hillsong United

You call me out upon the waters
The great unknown where feet may fail
And there I find You in the mystery
In oceans deep
My faith will stand

And I will call upon Your name
And keep my eyes above the waves
When oceans rise
My soul will rest in Your embrace
For I am Yours and You are mine

Your grace abounds in deepest waters
Your sovereign hand
Will be my guide
Where feet may fail and fear surrounds me
You've never failed and You won't start now

Spirit lead me where my trust is without borders
Let me walk upon the waters

Wherever You would call me
Take me deeper than my feet could ever wander
And my faith will be made stronger
In the presence of my Savior

I will call upon Your name
Keep my eyes above the waves
My soul will rest in Your embrace
I am Yours and You are mine

* * *

Hans

What I've learned:
1. Being kind is more important than being right.
2. There is always more than one perspective in a situation, and we have the option to choose a positive one.
3. What God brings us to, he will bring us through.
4. Happiness is shallow; peace has depth.
5. Never ask God why; ask for understanding of what is.
6. Love and accept people even when things don't go your way.
7. Forgive yourself, and don't worry so much about being forgiven.
8. Truly take it one day at a time, or even one minute at a time if necessary.
9. People's anger may be triggered by something I did or said, but the majority of the anger had already been built up inside them.
10. I can be happier with fewer material things and appreciate what I do have.
11. I need to remember the good that is in everyone and not just what appears on the surface.
12. An argument with family is better than silence alone.
13. I need humility because of my arrogance, I need acceptance for my defiance, and I need gratitude for my judgment.
14. Everyone makes other people happy. Some when they walk into a room and some when they leave it. We get to decide which one we want to be.
15. When people are ready, they change. They never do it before then, and sometimes they die before they get around to it. You can't make them change if they don't want to—just like when they do want to, you can't stop them.
16. Be the person who breaks the cycle. If you were judged, choose understanding. If you were rejected, choose acceptance. If you were shamed, choose compassion. Be the person you needed when you were hurting, not the

person who hurt you. Vow to be better than what broke you—to heal instead of becoming bitter so you act from your heart, not your pain.

17. Often God takes us through troubled waters not to drown us but to cleanse us.

18. Nobody dreams of growing up to be an alcoholic, an addict, divorced, broken, and depressed. Bad things happen to good people, the broken ones that always seem to have a vacancy in their hearts for those who would not even give a room in theirs.

19. Before you judge my life, my past, or my character— walk in my shoes, walk the path I have traveled, live my sorrow, my doubts, my fear, my pain, and my laughter. Remember: judge lest ye be judged. Everyone has their own story! When you have lived my life, you can judge!

20. Bad things are going to come regardless, but you have a choice on how you are going to deal with it.

21. Be there without judgment. Encourage, give purpose, and be the strength.

22. Life is all shades of gray; there are no absolutes

Jon and Hans

Giving back

* * *

Drifter Show Choir Champions 2018

Hannah and Delaney

I f you would have told us ten years ago—at the ages of eleven (Hannah) and nine (Delaney)—that one day our dad would be sober from alcohol, working two jobs, and counseling other addicts through their sobriety, we would have definitely looked you in the eyes and said you were crazy.

At first Mom liked to keep most stuff about Dad's addiction quiet and thought she could handle it and not get anyone involved. We didn't really know what was going on, but quickly we caught on. Mom was an angel and had to keep the house running while Dad would be drunk and when Mom got mad that he was drunk, he would leave and not come back for a few days. We never really knew where he went or how he somehow made it back home safely. We always felt like we were walking on eggshells because we never knew what Dad's state of mind would be when we came home from school. Will he be passed out drunk? Will he be sneaking around drinking? Will Mom be mad at him? Will there be fighting and yelling? Will he even be at home?

I (Hannah) will never forget going into the only bathroom in our apartment when I was thirteen and finding a plastic water bottle in the drawer. Opening it up, I smelled vodka. Exactly what I thought. I remember feeling my heart sink into my stomach. I dumped it down the drain and put the empty water bottle back in the drawer. I told Mom about it that first time, and she was mad at him. Then I would find myself going to the bathroom to purposefully look for a bottle of vodka to dump down the drain when I knew he had been drinking. I stopped telling Mom about finding the bottles because I didn't want to hear the fighting, but I knew getting rid of the alcohol was one way I could try to help the situation.

I (Delaney) will never forget the first time I feared my dad getting arrested. I was around twelve years old, and my sister (Hannah) and I were watching *Full House* in our parents' bedroom, which was in the basement of a bi-level house. My mom and dad were doing work around the house.

It was around 9:30 p.m. when all of a sudden we heard banging on the door. There were a couple of officers that came to the door to talk to my dad. My dad ignored the door, which led to them flashing their flashlights around the house, which was especially scary because they could see my sister and me still in the basement, and soon enough they barged in unexpectedly. My mom kept us safe in the basement while my dad talked to the officers. This was a tough time and opened my eyes to what a scary thing and toxic life my family and I were living. My mom made sure we were surrounded by friends who kept us out of the craziness that our life turned into. These friends are some of my lifelong friends who have helped me during the hard times of my dad's recovery. Over time, relationships flourished, and help was received. This all leads to the present day, where our family is better than ever and my dad is one of my best friends.

These are just a few moments of the hurt and heartbreak that we felt in the fight against our dad's addiction. People will tell you that addiction is a family disease, and we know firsthand that addiction is a disease that impacts everyone around the addict. But then God intervened. We were able to see a miracle work through with our dad's recovery because of Jesus.

One day in late October of 2014—when we were freshman in high school (Hannah) and in seventh grade (Delaney)—we went to school, and Mom went to work. So my dad woke up after a night of drinking, and he packed his bags, left his phone and wallet on the kitchen table, and left the house. We came home that day and had no idea where he went or where he was headed. This wasn't too out of the blue because had done this before but normally took his phone and would come home until later that night when we were all asleep, then he would apologize the next morning. It was a toxic cycle that affected the whole family.

Well, one day went past and no sign of our dad, then another day, then another day, and we still had not heard from him. My mom would repeat to us, "I can't control him, all we can do is pray for him." Every day he was gone. We were scared and worried, and the thought that we would never see our dad again was becoming more and more realistic.

Ten days passed before we heard anything. We had finally gotten a call that my dad was safe and in the hospital in Southern Indiana. Oh, what a relief. He is alive. We didn't see him again until March of 2015. He came home for a court date, and we got to spend the day as a family in Chicago. Our dad lived in a halfway home for six months where he attended a Baptist church before he moved back to the area where we were living. He has turned his life around and is the most loving, patient, and hardworking father. He puts me and Delaney as well as our mom before anything else in life. The rough times that our family went through have made us stronger and brought us closer to God.

Our dad's addiction has been the hardest thing our family has been through, but we believe God puts us through the scariest and darkest storms so that we can see and appreciate the rainbow on the other side. We want to share some words that we believe could help you in the midst of your own storm.

Hannah and Delaney 2021

God will be your umbrella and safe place in the storms of life. You don't feel like anyone else knows what you are going through, but we do, and they do. God knows. He sees you and hears you. Rely on him, and pray to him. Listen for his answers. Put your identity in Christ and him alone. God's way for your life will always surpass the plans you have on your own.

About the Authors

Lisa and Hans Scheller share their story of the challenges of marriage and raising a family when a partner becomes addicted to alcohol, hits bottom, and seeks recovery. You will learn how their fear turned to faith in God that eventually led them to keep their marriage intact while facing adversity in all areas of their lives. A testimony to how lives can be changed when God is the center of our lives

Lisa Scheller has been a Social Worker working as a Development Director for many non-profits. She is an entrepreneur and owner of Heart & Health. She is a certified Health Coach from the Institute for Integrative Nutrition, a Family Recovery Coach, Nutritional Recovery Coach and Relapse Coach from The Addictions Academy.

Hans Scheller has seven years of sobriety of alcohol addiction. Working on his own sobriety and recovery, he has been able to help many others who face the same demon. Hans is a Certified Peer Recovery Coach and has been mentoring addicts for two and half years.

We asked God for strength that we might achieve . . .
We were made weak so that we would learn to obey.
We asked God for material things so that we would be happy . . .
We were given poverty so that we may become wise.
We asked God for power so that we would have approval . . .
We were made weak so we would feel the need for God.
We got nothing we asked for but more than we hoped for.
We are richly BLESSED!

Made in the USA
Middletown, DE
04 July 2022